HOME SKILLS

Building Decks

ALL THE INFORMATION YOU NEED TO DESIGN & BUILD YOUR OWN DECK

COOL
SPRINGS
PRESS
Home and Garden Experts™

MINNEAPOLIS, MINNESOTA

CONTENTS

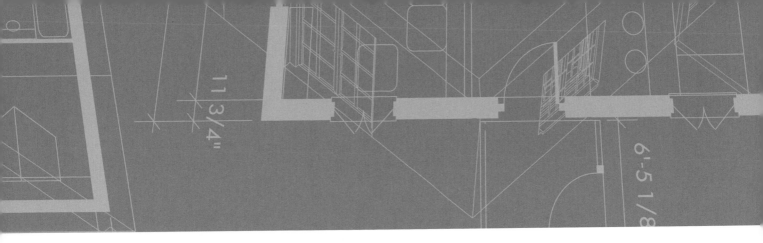

Deck Construction

Finishing Decks

Resources

Introduction

A DECK IS MANY THINGS, and a well-planned deck project can transform your home in so many ways. A deck can serve as a transition from yard to house, creating a room that is outside. A deck can add space to a yard by flattening out a slope to create a functional area. A deck can add space to a house by providing a dirt-free outdoor living space. Decks can be used for relaxation, entertainment, or even storage.

Decks come in all shapes and sizes—they can be as simple as an octagon only inches above the ground or as complex as a multi-level cascade flowing down two or three stories. It can look sleek and modern or weathered and full of character.

The good news about decks is that the construction skills necessary for a simple platform deck are quite basic. And, the skills needed for a complex

deck are not that much more advanced. *HomeSkills: Building Decks* contains all the information you need to plan and construct the most popular walkout decks complete with railings and stairs. All aspects are covered from planning and working with building inspectors, to pouring concrete footings, decking options, curved railings, and tree cutouts.

The main issue in deck building is planning and following the very specific building codes for decks. These building codes are important because decks are often places where people congregate. No one wants a party to end with revelers on their way to the emergency room because proper building rules were not followed. If a deck is constructed properly and fully according to code, those accidents are unlikely to happen.

DECK BASICS

ONE OF THE BENEFITS of building a deck is that you can create an impressive structure in a relatively short period of time, even with modest tools and skills. It's an exciting project to undertake, but don't let your energy and enthusiasm get the best of you. Without careful planning and design on the front end, your deck project could be frustrating to build, unnecessarily costly, or even dangerous to use when you're through. So, in order to put your best foot forward, plan to spend those first hours of the project at a desk developing a thorough plan.

As you begin the planning process, keep in mind that your deck needs to satisfy four goals: it should meet the functional needs of your household, contribute to your home's curb appeal and property value, fit your project budget, and satisfy local building codes for appearance, location, and safety. This chapter will help familiarize you with building codes and deck materials so you can build confidently and correctly, the first time.

DECK BUILDING CODES

Most decks are relatively simple structures, but even a basic deck project must conform to the requirements of building codes in your area. In fact, virtually every aspect of your new deck—from its location on your property, to the design you choose and the materials you buy to build it—must meet stringent guidelines for safety. Codes vary to some degree from state to state, but they are based on general regulations established by the International Residential Code.

Your local building inspector can provide you with a list of the relevant deck codes and help you interpret them so you can create code-compliant plans for your deck project.

The next few pages will provide a survey of some of the more common code requirements for decks, although it is by no means comprehensive. Use this section as a way to familiarize yourself with the code requirements you will probably face as you plan and build your new deck.

Metal flashings must be used to prevent moisture from penetrating between the ledger and the wall.

Beams may overhang posts by no more than 1 foot. Building regulations generally require that beams should rest on top of or be fully notched into posts, secured with metal post-beam caps or bolts.

Footing diameter and depth is determined by your local codes, based on the estimated load of the deck and on the composition of your soil. In regions with cold winters, footings must extend a prescribed depth below the frost line. Minimum diameter for concrete footings is 8".

Tip

You may want to download a free PDF copy of the "Prescriptive Residential Deck Construction Guide" from the American Wood Council at www.awc.org. In addition, many communities publish local building codes on their websites.

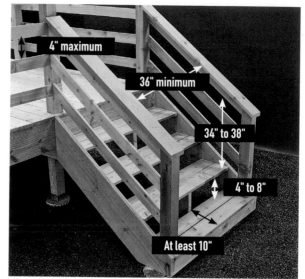

Railings are required by local codes for decks more than 30" above the ground and must usually be at least 36" in height. Bottom rails must be positioned with no more than 4" of open space below them. Balusters, whether vertical or horizontal, can be spaced no more than 4" apart.

Stairs must be at least 36" wide. Vertical step risers must be between 4" and 7¾" and uniform in height within a staircase. Treads must have a horizontal run of at least 10" and be uniform in size within a staircase. Stair railings should be 34" to 38" above the noses of the step treads, and there should be no more than 6" of space between the bottom rail and the steps. The space between the rails or balusters should be no more than 4". Note: Grippable handrails may be required for decks with four or more risers. Consult your local building inspector.

Code violation. The International Building Code no longer allows joists to straddle the sides of a post fastened with through bolts, as shown here. It no longer endorses structural posts made of 4 × 4 lumber: 6 × 6 is the minimum size. Railing posts may be 4 × 4.

Beam assemblies. Deck beams made of 2× lumber must be fastened together with staggered rows of 10d galvanized common nails or 3" deck screws. If the wood components that make up the beam are spliced together, stagger the splices and locate them over beams for added strength.

Engineered beams, such as a laminated wood product or steel girder, should be used on decks with very long joist spans, where standard dimension lumber is not adequate for the load. Engineered beams for decks must be rated for exterior use.

Post-to-beam attachment. Deck posts, regardless of length or size of deck, should be made of minimum 6 × 6 structural lumber. Notch the posts so that beams can bear fully in the notch, and attach them with pairs of ½-in.-diameter galvanized through bolts and washers. Or, you can mount beams on top of posts with galvanized post cap hardware. Some codes prohibit the use of notched posts. Check with your local building department.

Ledgers and rim joists. When a ledger is fastened to a rim joist, the house siding must be removed prior to installation. Either ½-in.-diameter lag screws or through-bolts with washers can be used to make the connections.

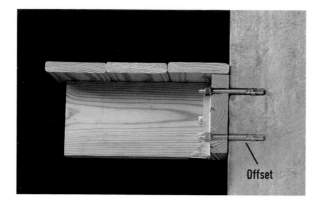

Ledgers and concrete walls. Ledgers fastened to solid concrete must be attached with bolts and washers driven into approved expansion, epoxy, or adhesive anchors.

Ledgers and block walls. When fastening ledgers to hollow concrete block walls, secure the attachment bolts to the wall with approved epoxy anchors (also called acrylic anchors).

No notched railing posts. Code no longer allows deck railing posts to be notched where they attach to the deck rim joists. Railing posts should be fastened to rim joists with pairs of ½-in.-diameter through bolts and washers. In some cases, hold-down anchor hardware may also be required.

Stair lighting. Deck stairs must be illuminated at night from a light located at the top of the landing. The light can be switch-controlled from inside the house, motion-controlled, or used in conjunction with a timer switch.

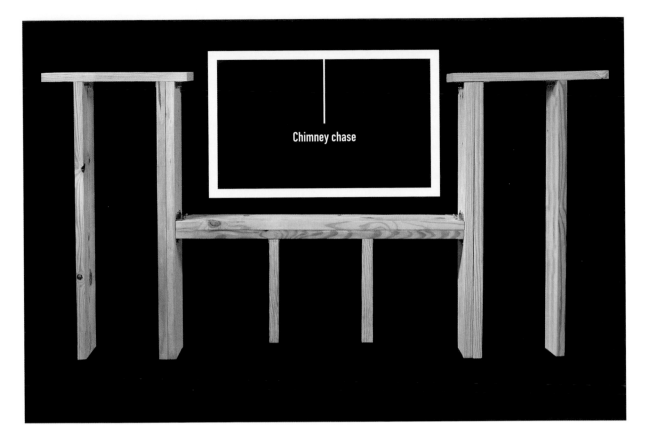

Chimney chase

Chimney chases and bays. When framing a deck around a chimney or bay window, a suitable double header must be added where the ledger is spliced to accommodate the obstruction. The type of header shown here can span a maximum of 6 ft.

Rim joist connections. Attach rim joists to the end of each joist with five #10 × 3-in. minimum wood screws. Secure decking to the top of rim joists with #10 × 3-in. minimum wood screws, two per board.

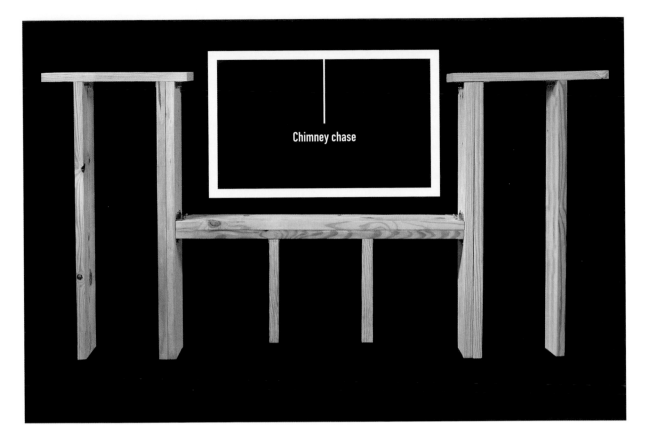

DETERMINING LUMBER SIZE

A deck has seven major structural parts: the ledger, decking, joists, one or more beams, posts, stairway stringers, and stairway treads. To create a working design plan and choose the correct lumber size, you must know the span limits of each part of the deck. The ledger is attached directly to the house and does not have a span limit.

A span limit is the safe distance a board can cross without support from underneath. The maximum safe span depends on the size and wood species of the board. For example, 2 × 6 southern pine joists spaced 16 inches on-center can safely span 9 feet 9 inches, while 2 × 10 joists can span 16 feet 1 inch.

Begin planning your deck by first choosing the size and pattern for the decking. Determine the actual layout of joists and beams by using the tables on the opposite page and information in the "Prescriptive Residential Deck Construction Guide" available at www.awc.org. In general, a deck designed with larger lumber, such as 2 × 12 joists and beams, requires fewer pieces because the boards have a longer span limit. Finally, choose the stair and railing lumber that fits your plan, using the same tables.

Use the design plans to make a complete list of the quantities of each lumber size your deck requires. Add 10 percent to compensate for lumber flaws and construction errors. Full-service lumberyards have extensive selections of lumber, but prices may be higher than those at home improvement centers.

Nominal vs. Actual Lumber Dimensions:
When planning a deck, remember that the actual size of lumber is smaller than the nominal size by which lumber is sold. Use the actual dimensions when drawing a deck design plan.

Nominal	Actual
1 x 4	¾" x 3½"
5/4 x 6	1" x 5½"
2 x 4	1½" x 3½"
2 x 6	1½" x 5½"
2 x 8	1½" x 7¼"
2 x 10	1½" x 9¼"
2 x 12	1½" x 11¼"
4 x 4	3½" x 3½"
6 x 6	5¼" x 5¼"

Tip
The quality of lumber at home centers can vary. You can inspect the wood and hand-pick the pieces you want or add a larger percentage to compensate for lumber flaws. Both lumberyards and home centers will deliver lumber for a small fee, and you can usually return unused, uncut lumber if you keep your receipts.

CHART 1: MAXIMUM SPANS FOR VARIOUS JOIST SIZES

Size	Southern Pine			Ponderosa Pine			Western Cedar		
	12" OC	16" OC	24" OC	12" OC	16" OC	24" OC	12" OC	16" OC	24" OC
2 × 6	10 ft. 9"	9 ft. 9"	8 ft. 6"	9 ft. 2"	8 ft. 4"	7 ft. 0"	9 ft. 2"	8 ft. 4"	7 ft. 3"
2 × 8	14 ft. 2"	12 ft. 10"	11 ft. 0"	12 ft. 1"	10 ft. 10"	8 ft. 10"	12 ft. 1"	11 ft. 0"	9 ft. 2"
2 × 10	18 ft. 0"	16 ft. 1"	13 ft. 5"	15 ft. 4"	13 ft. 3"	10 ft. 10"	15 ft. 5"	13 ft. 9"	11 ft. 3"
2 × 12	21 ft. 9"	19 ft. 0"	15 ft. 4"	17 ft. 9"	15 ft. 5"	12 ft. 7"	18 ft. 5"	16 ft. 5"	13 ft. 0"

DIMENSION & SPAN LIMIT TABLES FOR DECK LUMBER

Recommended Decking Span Between Joists:
Decking boards can be made from a variety of lumber sizes. For a basic deck use 2 × 4 or 2 × 6 lumber with joists spaced 16 inches apart.

Decking Boards	Max Span
5/4 x 4 or 5/4 x 6, laid straight	6"
5/4 x 4 or 5/4 x 6, laid diagonal	12"
5/4 x 6 composite, laid straight	12"
5/4 x 6 composite, laid diagonal	See manu. specs
2 x 4 or 2 x 6, laid straight	16"
2 x 4 or 2 x 6, laid diagonal	12"
2 x 4, laid on edge	24"

Minimum Stair Stringer Sizes: Size of stair stringers depends on the span of the stairway. For example, if the bottom of the stairway lies 7 feet from the deck, build the stringers from 2 × 12s. Stringers should be spaced no more than 36 inches apart. Use of a center stringer is recommended for stairways with more than three steps.

Span of Stairway	Stringer Size
Up to 6 ft.	2 x 10
More than 6 ft.	2 x 12

Recommended Railing Sizes: Sizes of posts, rails, and caps depend on the spacing of the railing posts. For example, if railing posts are spaced 6 feet apart, use 4 × 4 posts and 2 × 6 rails and caps.

Space Between	Post Size	Cap Size	Rail Size
2 ft. to 3 ft.	2 x 4	2 x 4	2 x 4
3 ft. to 4 ft.	4 x 4	2 x 4	2 x 4
4 ft. to 6 ft.	4 x 4	2 x 6	2 x 6

Meet or exceed all lumber size codes. For example, use lumber that is at least 6 × 6" for all deck posts, regardless of the size of the deck or the length of the post.

Tip
Composite, plastic, and aluminum decking all have their own span specifications, which are shorter than the standardized specifications for lumber. Always consult the manufacturer's recommendations when using non-wood decking. None of these materials are suitable for use in structural support.

UNDERSTANDING LOADS

The supporting structural members of a deck—the posts, beams, and joists—must be sturdy enough to easily support the heaviest anticipated load on the deck. They must not only carry the substantial weight of the surface decking and railings, but also the weight of people, deck furnishings, and, in some climates, snow.

The charts and diagrams shown here will help you plan a deck so the size and spacing of the structural members are sufficient to support the load, assuming normal use. These recommendations are followed in most regions, but you should still check with your local building official for regulations that are unique to your area. In cases where the deck will support a hot tub or pool, you must consult your local building inspections office for load guidelines.

When choosing lumber for the structural members of your deck, select the diagram below that best matches your deck design, then follow the advice for applying the charts on the opposite page. Since different species of wood have different strengths, make sure to use the entries that match the type of lumber sold by your building center. When selecting the size for concrete footings, make sure to consider the composition of your soil; dense soils require footings with a larger diameter.

Post-and-beam deck: Using Chart 1, determine the proper size for your joists, based on the on-center (OC) spacing between joists and the overall length, or span, of the joists (A). For example, if you will be using southern pine joists to span a 12-ft. distance, you can use 2 × 8 lumber spaced no more than 16" apart, or 2 × 10 lumber spaced no more than 24" apart. Once you have determined allowable joist sizes, use Chart 2 to determine an appropriate beam size, post spacing, and footing size for your deck.

Cantilevered deck: Use the distance from the ledger to the beam (A) to determine minimum joist size, and use A + (2 × B) when choosing beam and footing sizes. For example, if your deck measures 9 ft. from ledger to beam, with an additional 3-ft. cantilevered overhang, use 9 ft. to choose a joist size from Chart 1 (2 × 6 southern pine joists spaced 16" apart, or

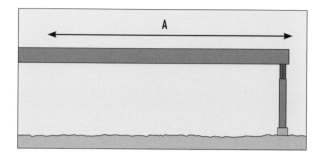

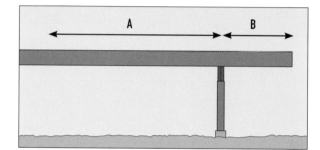

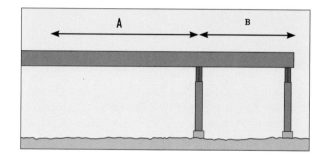

2 × 8 joists spaced 24" apart). Then, use A + (2 × B), or 15 ft., to find an appropriate beam size, post spacing, and footing size from Chart 2. If your deck cantilevers more than 18" beyond the support beam, add 1" to the recommended diameter for footings.

Multiple-beam deck: Use distance A or B, whichever is larger, when determining joist size from Chart 1. For example, if your deck measures 8 ft. to beam #1 and another 4 ft. to beam #2, you can use 2 × 6 southern pine joists. Referring to Chart 2, use the total distance A + B to determine the size of beam #1, the spacing for the posts, and the size of the footings. Use joist length B to determine the size of beam #2, the post spacing, and footing size. For example, with an overall span of 12 ft. (8 ft. to the first beam, 4 ft. to the second), beam #1 could be made from two southern pine 2 × 8s; beam #2, from two 2 × 6s.

CHART 2: DIAMETERS FOR POST FOOTING (INCHES)

Post Spacing

Joist Length (left axis)

Joist Length		4'	5'	6'	7'	8'	9'	10'	11'	12'
6'	Southern Pine Beam	1–2×6	1–2×6	1–2×6	2–2×6	2–2×6	2–2×6	2–2×8	2–2×8	2–2×10
	Ponderosa Pine Beam	1–2×6	1–2×6	1–2×8	2–2×8	2–2×8	2–2×8	2–2×10	2–2×10	2–2×12
	Corner Footing	6 5 4	7 6 5	7 6 5	8 7 6	9 7 6	9 7 6	10 8 7	10 8 7	10 9 7
	Intermediate Footing	9 8 7	10 8 7	10 9 7	11 9 8	12 10 9	13 10 9	14 11 10	14 12 10	15 12 10
7'	Southern Pine Beam	1–2×6	1–2×6	1–2×6	2–2×6	2–2×6	2–2×8	2–2×8	2–2×10	2–2×10
	Ponderosa Pine Beam	1–2×6	1–2×6	1–2×8	2–2×8	2–2×8	2–2×10	2–2×10	2–2×10	2–2×12
	Corner Footing	7 5 5	7 6 5	8 7 6	9 7 6	9 8 7	10 8 7	10 8 7	11 9 8	11 9 8
	Intermediate Footing	9 8 7	10 8 7	11 9 8	12 10 9	13 11 9	14 11 10	15 12 10	15 13 11	16 13 11
8'	Southern Pine Beam	1–2×6	1–2×6	2–2×6	2–2×6	2–2×8	2–2×8	2–2×8	2–2×10	2–2×10
	Ponderosa Pine Beam	1–2×6	2–2×6	2–2×8	2–2×8	2–2×8	2–2×10	2–2×10	2–2×10	3–2×10
	Corner Footing	7 6 5	8 6 6	9 7 6	9 8 7	10 8 7	10 8 7	11 9 8	11 9 8	12 10 9
	Intermediate Footing	10 8 7	11 9 8	12 10 9	13 11 9	14 11 10	15 12 10	16 13 11	16 13 12	17 14 12
9'	Southern Pine Beam	1–2×6	1–2×6	2–2×6	2–2×6	2–2×8	2–2×8	2–2×10	2–2×10	2–2×12
	Ponderosa Pine Beam	1–2×6	2–2×6	2–2×8	2–2×8	2–2×10	2–2×10	2–2×10	3–2×10	3–2×10
	Corner Footing	7 6 5	8 7 6	9 7 6	10 8 7	10 9 7	11 9 8	12 10 8	12 10 9	13 10 9
	Intermediate Footing	10 9 7	12 10 8	13 10 9	14 11 10	15 12 10	16 13 11	17 14 12	17 14 12	18 15 13
10'	Southern Pine Beam	1–2×6	1–2×6	2–2×6	2–2×6	2–2×8	2–2×8	2–2×10	2–2×12	2–2×12
	Ponderosa Pine Beam	1–2×6	1–2×6	2–2×8	2–2×8	2–2×10	2–2×10	2–2×12	3–2×10	3–2×12
	Corner Footing	8 6 6	9 7 6	10 8 7	10 8 7	11 9 8	12 10 8	12 10 9	13 11 9	14 11 10
	Intermediate Footing	11 9 8	12 10 9	14 11 10	15 12 10	16 13 11	17 14 12	17 14 12	18 15 13	19 16 14
11'	Southern Pine Beam	1–2×6	2–2×6	2–2×6	2–2×8	2–2×8	2–2×10	2–2×10	2–2×12	2–2×12
	Ponderosa Pine Beam	2–2×6	2–2×6	2–2×8	2–2×8	2–2×10	2–2×12	2–2×12	3–2×10	3–2×12
	Corner Footing	8 7 6	9 7 6	10 8 7	11 9 8	12 9 8	12 10 9	13 11 9	14 11 10	14 12 10
	Intermediate Footing	12 9 8	13 11 9	14 12 10	15 12 10	16 13 11	17 14 12	17 14 12	18 15 13	19 16 14
12'	Southern Pine Beam	1–2×6	2–2×6	2–2×6	2–2×8	2–2×8	2–2×10	2–2×10	2–2×12	3–2×10
	Ponderosa Pine Beam	2–2×6	2–2×6	2–2×8	2–2×10	2–2×10	2–2×12	2–2×12	3–2×12	3–2×12
	Corner Footing	9 7 6	10 8 7	10 9 7	11 9 8	12 10 9	13 10 9	14 11 10	14 12 10	15 12 10
	Intermediate Footing	12 10 9	14 11 10	15 12 10	16 13 11	17 14 12	18 15 13	19 16 14	20 16 14	21 17 15
13'	Southern Pine Beam	1–2×6	2–2×6	2–2×6	2–2×8	2–2×8	2–2×10	2–2×10	2–2×12	3–2×10
	Ponderosa Pine Beam	2–2×6	2–2×6	2–2×8	2–2×10	2–2×12	2–2×12	2–2×12	3–2×12	3–2×12
	Corner Footing	9 7 6	10 8 7	11 9 8	12 10 8	13 10 9	13 11 9	14 12 10	15 12 10	15 13 11
	Intermediate Footing	13 10 9	14 12 10	15 13 11	17 14 12	18 15 13	19 15 13	20 16 14	21 17 15	22 18 15
14'	Southern Pine Beam	1–2×6	2–2×6	2–2×6	2–2×8	2–2×10	2–2×10	2–2×12	3–2×10	3–2×12
	Ponderosa Pine Beam	2–2×6	2–2×8	2–2×8	2–2×10	2–2×12	3–2×10	3–2×12	3–2×12	Eng Bm
	Corner Footing	9 8 7	10 8 7	11 9 8	12 10 9	13 11 9	14 11 10	15 12 10	15 13 11	16 13 11
	Intermediate Footing	13 11 9	15 12 10	16 13 11	17 14 12	18 15 13	20 16 14	21 17 15	22 18 15	23 18 16
15'	Southern Pine Beam	2–2×6	2–2×6	2–2×8	2–2×8	2–2×10	2–2×12	2–2×12	3–2×10	3–2×12
	Ponderosa Pine Beam	2–2×6	2–2×8	2–2×8	2–2×10	3–2×10	3–2×10	3–2×12	3–2×12	Eng Bm
	Corner Footing	10 8 7	11 9 8	12 10 8	13 10 9	14 11 10	14 12 10	15 12 11	16 13 11	17 14 12
	Intermediate Footing	14 11 10	15 12 11	17 14 12	18 15 13	19 16 14	20 17 14	21 17 15	22 18 16	23 19 17

Legend:

	Clay	Sand	Gravel
(Corner)	10	8	7
(Intermediate)	14	11	10

Soil composition: Clay Sand Gravel

DEVELOPING YOUR DECK PLAN

A deck plan is more than just measured drawings. It needs to account for your deck's functional purposes as well as its dimensional form. Before you begin drawing plans, determine everything you want your deck to include. Here's where you'll focus on functional concerns. The size, shape, and location of your deck can be affected by several questions: Will the deck be used for entertaining? Will you cook on it? Do you need privacy? Consider how the features of the house and yard influence the deck design. Weather, time of day, and seasonal changes affect deck usage. For example, if your deck will be used mainly for summertime evening meals, look at the sun, shade, and wind patterns on the planned site during this time of day.

Of course, building plans also help you estimate lumber and hardware needs, and provide the measurements needed to lay out the deck and cut the lumber. You will need two types of drawings for your deck plans and to obtain a building permit. A plan view shows the parts of the deck as they are viewed from directly overhead. An elevation shows the deck parts as viewed from the side or front.

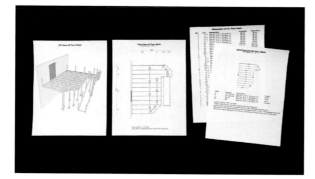

Many building centers will help you design and create deck plan drawings if you purchase your lumber and other deck materials from them. Their design capabilities include determining a detailed lumber and materials list based on the exact deck plan created.

Calculator Conversion Chart

As a carpenter you will measure in eighths and sixteenths. But your calculator works in tenths and hundredths. Here's a handy chart to help you convert back and forth.

8ths	16ths	Decimal
	1	.0625
1	2	.125
	3	.1875
2	4	.25
	5	.3125
3	6	.375
	7	.4375
4	8	.5
	9	.5625
5	10	.625
	11	.6875
6	12	.75
	13	.8125
7	14	.875
	15	.9375
8	16	1

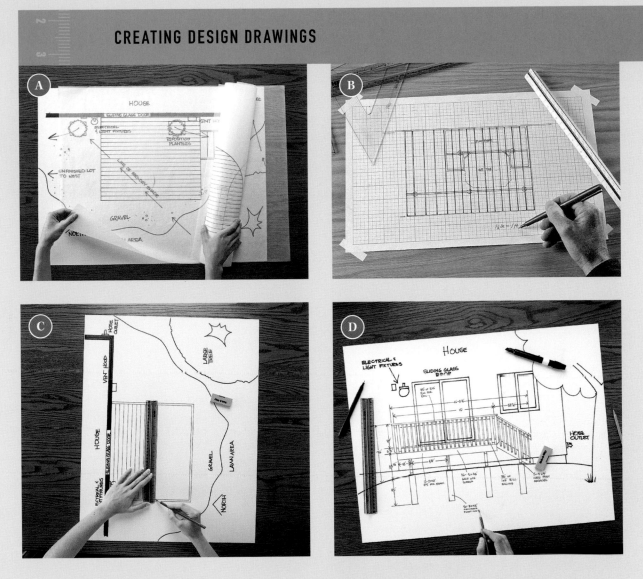

A   Use tracing paper to sketch different deck layouts. Then, test your ideas by overlaying the deck sketches onto a drawing of your building site. Make sure to consider sun patterns and the locations of existing landscape features when developing a deck plan. Adapt an existing deck plan, either borrowed from a book or magazine, or purchased in blueprint form. Tracing paper, pens, and measuring tools are all you need to revise an existing deck plan.

B   Use drafting tools and graph paper if you are creating a deck plan from scratch. Use a generous scale, such as 1" equals 1 ft., that allows you to illustrate the deck in fine detail. Remember to create both overhead plan drawings and side elevation drawings of your project.

C   To avoid confusion, do not try to show all parts of the deck in a single plan view, especially for a complicated or multi-level deck. First, draw one plan view that shows the deck outline and the pattern of the decking boards. Then make another plan view (or more) that shows the underlying ledger, joists, beams, and posts.

D   Elevation drawings must include deck dimensions, size and type of hardware to be used, beam sizes (if visible in drawing), and footing locations and their dimensions. Also indicate the grade of the ground in the deck area. Make multiple elevation drawings if necessary for complicated or multi-level decks.

WORKING WITH BUILDING INSPECTORS

In most regions, you must have your plans reviewed and approved by a building official if your deck is attached to a permanent structure or if it is more than 30 inches high. The building official makes sure that your planned deck meets building code requirements for safe construction.

These pages show some of the most common code requirements for decks. But before you design your project, check with the building inspection division of your city office, since code regulations can vary from area to area. A valuable source of planning information, the building official may provide you with a free information sheet outlining the relevant requirements.

Once you have completed your deck plans, return to the building inspections office and have the official review them. Make certain you know how many copies of the plans they require before you go. If your plans meet code, you will be issued a building permit, usually for a small fee. This process often takes a few days. Regulations may require that a field inspector review the deck at specified stages in the building process. If so, make sure to allow for the review schedule in your project schedule.

Plan-approval Checklist

When the building official reviews your deck plans, he or she will look for the following details. Make sure your plan drawings include all this information.

- Overall size and shape of the deck.

- Position of the deck relative to buildings, property lines, and setbacks. Generally, a deck must be at least 5 ft. from the property line, although this varies locality to locality.

- Location of all beams and posts.

- Detailed drawings of joinery methods for all structural members of the deck.

- Size and on-center (OC) spacing of joists.

- Height of deck above grade.

- Thickness of deck boards—or profile of composite decking.

- Type of soil that will support the concrete post footings: sand, loam, or clay.

- Species of wood to be used, and/or type of composite material.

- Types of metal connectors and other hardware you plan to use in constructing the deck.

- Lighting and other electrical outlets or fixtures that will be wired into the deck.

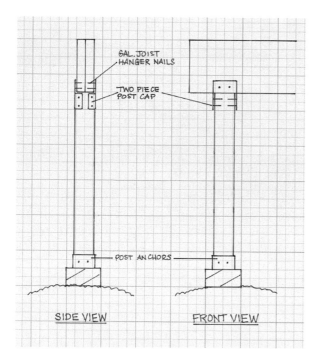

Draw detailed illustrations of the joinery methods you plan to use for all structural members of your deck. Your building official will want to see details on post-footing connections, post-beam joints, beam-joist joints, and ledger connections. Be prepared to make adjustments.

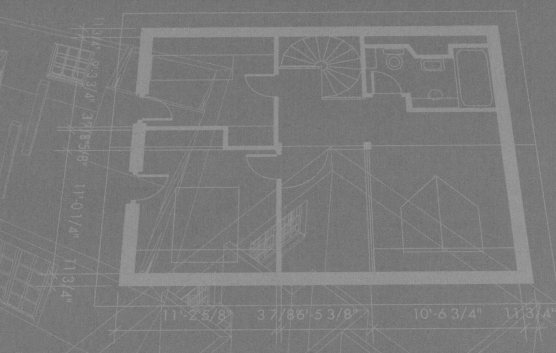

DECK MATERIALS

FOOTINGS & STRUCTURAL LUMBER

Generally, pressure-treated lumber is the preferred choice for deck posts, beams, and joist framing. It offers good resistance to decay and insect infestation, it's widely available in most parts of the country and it's a cheaper alternative to other rot-resistant wood species such as cedar or redwood. Treated lumber is milled in 4 × 4, 4 × 6, and 6 × 6 sizes for posts. Larger dimensions are available by special order. You'll need 2× treated lumber for beams and joists. Joists are usually 2 × 8 or larger. If your deck is particularly large or designed with oversized spans, you may need to use engineered beams instead of building beams from treated lumber. Make sure your engineered beams are rated for exterior use. Check the grade stamps or the stapled tags on your pressure-treated posts; they should be approved to a level of .40 retention for ground contact.

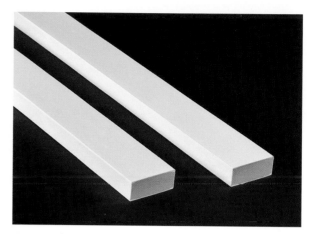

Composite lumber is widely used for non-structural purposes such as decking, skirting, and railing. Made from sawdust, recycled plastic, and binders, composite lumber is available in solid, hollow, and other profiles.

Engineered beams that are rated for exterior use are a sturdy alternative to beams made from 2× lumber. They may be required if you are building a large deck with expansive or unusual spans. Your building inspector will help you make this determination.

Treated lumber is available in common nominal sizes for use as deck beams and joists. The Chemical formulations of pressure-treated lumber are alkaline copper quaternary (ACQ) and copper boron azole (CBA). Both ACQ and CBA provide wood with the same protection from decay and insect attack. However these treatments are corrosive to metals. Make sure to choose fasteners and connective hardware that are approved for use with ACQ- and CBA-treated lumber.

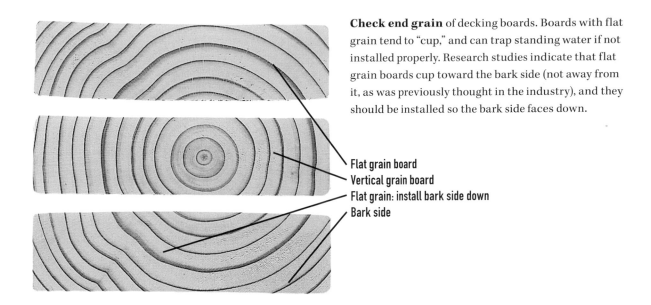

Check end grain of decking boards. Boards with flat grain tend to "cup," and can trap standing water if not installed properly. Research studies indicate that flat grain boards cup toward the bark side (not away from it, as was previously thought in the industry), and they should be installed so the bark side faces down.

Flat grain board
Vertical grain board
Flat grain: install bark side down
Bark side

Tip

Select the flattest structural lumber you can find, free of splits, checks, and large loose knots. To prevent warping, stack and store it in a dry place or cover it with a tarp until you need it.

Tip: Sealing End Grain

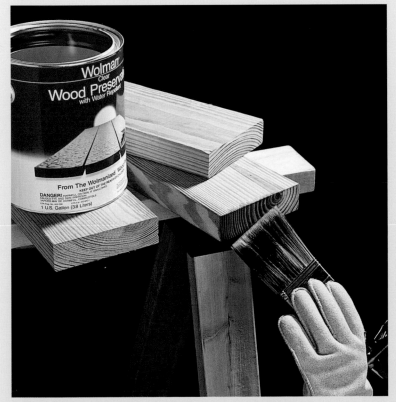

Seal cut edges of all lumber, including pressure-treated wood, by brushing on clear liquid sealer-preservative. Chemicals used in pressure treatment do not always penetrate completely. Sealer-preservative protects all types of wood from rot.

WOOD DECKING

Wood continues to be the most popular choice among decking materials, due in large part to price. Pressure-treated decking remains the least expensive deck option, but other types of hardwoods and softwoods feature unique grain pattern and coloring that makes them consistently desirable. Wood of all types is easy to work with, and most softwoods take stain or paint well, allowing you to alter the appearance almost at will.

The two most popular choices for wood decking are pressure-treated and cedar. Depending on where you live, you may have other options as well. Redwood may still be available if you live on the West Coast, and cypress is common in the South. Redwood, cypress, and cedar are naturally resistant to decay and insects, which makes them excellent choices for decking.

If cost is less important than quality, you might consider covering your deck with mahogany, ipê, or any of several other exotic hardwoods grouped under the term "ironwood"—so-called because their cell structures are so dense the woods will sink in water.

Tip

Naturally decay-resistant lumbers can be left unfinished to weather to a silvery gray color in a few years. However, the lifespan of the wood will be increased if you apply some sort of finish.

For pressure-treated or cedar decking, you'll have to select a thickness that works for your budget and design. One option is to use 2× lumber. It will span wider joist spacing without flexing, but generally 2× lumber is made from lower-grade material that may contain more natural defects. Another choice is to use 5/4 decking, pronounced "five quarter." Its actual dry thickness is 1 inch and the edges are radiused to help minimize splinters. Often, 5/4 lumber is clearer than 2× lumber, but it's not as stiff. You may need to space your joists more closely with 5/4 decking. Either way, you can commonly find 2× or 5/4 decking in lengths up to 16 or even 20 feet at most home centers.

Ipê

Cedar

Pressure-treated pine

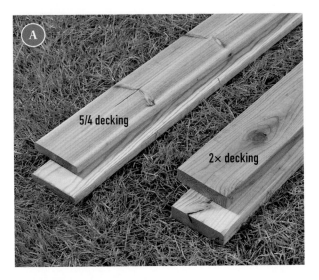

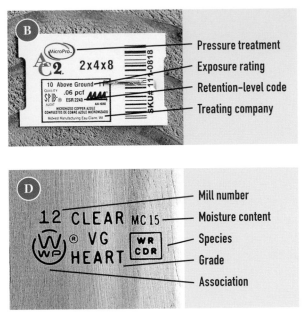

Pressure treatment

Exposure rating

Retention-level code

Treating company

Mill number

Moisture content

Species

Grade

Association

Waney

Knotty

Split

Warped

A Both 2× and 5/4 lumber are suitable for use as decking. However, 5/4 will generally be of higher quality, and the radiused edges prevent splintering—an important consideration for bare feet or if you have young children.

B Pressure-treated lumber stamps list the type of preservative and the chemical retention level, as well as the exposure rating and the name and location of the treating company.

C Be picky about the quality of the decking you buy. Natural defects in the wood could make the piece harder to install or deteriorate prematurely. Watch for soft pockets of sap in the wood. Sap will get sticky in warm weather, and the resin can bleed through wood finishes, leaving brown stains.

D Cedar grade stamps list the mill number, moisture content, species, lumber grade, and membership association. Western red cedar (WRC) or incense cedar (INC) for decks should be heartwood (HEART) with a maximum moisture content of 15% (MC15).

NON-WOOD DECKING

Decking made from non-wood materials such as composite lumber and PVC has taken over a large share of the decking market in recent years. Composite decking has only been around for a few decades, but it's a compelling option to consider for your deck. Most forms of composite decking are made from a blend of post-consumer plastic waste and wood pulp or non-wood fibers. The plastic component—polyethylene or polypropylene—makes the material impervious to rotting, and insects don't like it. Unlike solid wood, it has no grain, so it won't splinter or crack, and there are no knots or natural defects to cut away. Other formulations of synthetic decking contain no wood at all. These are made from polyethylene, PVC, polystyrene, or fiberglass blends.

When composite lumber first hit the market, it didn't look anything like wood, and color choices were limited. Now, it's available in a range of wood textures and colors. Most products are non-toxic, easy to cut, drill, and fasten, and do not require finishing. Maintenance is usually limited to an occasional cleaning or spot removal. However, composite decking is more flexible than wood, so you may need to use closer joist spacing in your deck design. It's also heavier than wood and generally more expensive.

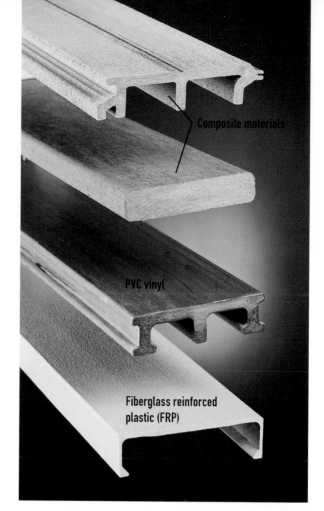

Composite materials

PVC vinyl

Fiberglass reinforced plastic (FRP)

Tip
Composite decking comes with impressive warranties, which may last from 10 years to a lifetime, depending on the product. Some warranties are transferable from one homeowner to the next.

Composite and other non-wood decking often require special fasteners that are designed to reduce "mushrooming" that occurs when the decking material bulges up around the screwhead. Pilot holes are recommended for some types as well.

Composite decking colors cover the spectrum of wood tones, plus grays and white. The color is continuous throughout the material, but exposure to strong, direct sunlight may cause the surface color to fade. Surface patterns and textures of composite decking range from virtually smooth to intricate wood grain styles. Patterns and textures vary by manufacturer, but many offer varieties that convincingly mimic species of wood.

While composite decking can be fastened down conventionally with screws, you may be able to use various edge-fastening systems instead to avoid driving screws through the board faces.

Composite Materials

Composite materials blend together wood fibers and recycled plastics to create a rigid product that, unlike wood, will not rot, splinter, warp, or crack. Painting or staining is unnecessary. Like wood, these deck boards can be cut to size, using a circular saw with a large-tooth blade.

PVC vinyl and plastic decking materials are shipped in kits that contain everything necessary to install the decking other than the deck screws. The kits are preordered to size, usually in multiples of the combined width of a deck board and the fasteners. The drawback of PVC vinyl decking is that it expands and contracts with freeze/thaw cycles.

Fiberglass reinforced plastic (FRP) decking will last a lifetime. Manufacturers claim that the material is three times as strong as wood and not affected by heat, sunlight, or severe weather. The decking is preordered to size, but if necessary, it can be cut using a circular saw with a diamond-tip or masonry blade.

FASTENERS

Certain structural connections of your deck will require the use of lag screws, through bolts, and concrete anchors to withstand the heavy loads and sheer forces applied to a deck. Be sure to use hot-dipped galvanized or stainless steel hardware to prevent rusting or corrosion from pressure-treating chemicals.

Here is an overview of the anchoring fasteners you may need for your project.

Tip

Building codes require that you install a washer beneath the heads of lag screws or bolts and another washer before attaching nuts. Washers prevent fasteners from tearing through wood and secure hardware under stress.

Galvanized or stainless steel lag screws and washers are the correct fasteners for installing ledgers to the band joist of a house. You can also use them for making other wood-to-wood connections.

Fasteners for Anchoring

Use ½"-diameter or larger through bolts, washers, and nuts for fastening beams to posts or railing posts to joists. They should be galvanized or made of stainless steel for corrosion resistance.

J-bolts, embedded in the wet concrete of deck footings, provide a secure connection for attaching concrete footings to metal connecting hardware.

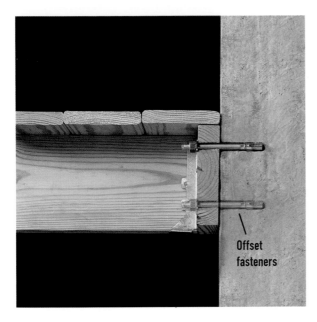

Offset
fasteners

Wedge or sleeve anchors draw a wedge through a hollow sleeve, expanding it to form a tight fit in solid concrete. A nut on the threaded end holds the ledger boards in place.

A bolt driven through the foundation from the inside can be fitted with a washer and nut to secure the ledger.

Soft metal shield anchors expand when lag screws are driven into them. They make suitable connections in either solid concrete or hollow block foundations.

High strength epoxy and threaded rod are good options for attaching metal connecting hardware to concrete footings.

METAL CONNECTORS

Sheet-metal connecting hardware comes in assorted shapes and styles. It is used to create strong wood-to-wood or wood-to-concrete joints quickly and easily. For instance, metal post anchors not only provide a simple way to attach posts and footings, they also create space between the two surfaces so post ends stay dry. Joist hangers are a fast way to hang long, heavy joists accurately. Post beam caps, T-straps, and angled joist hangers are ideal solutions for building stacked joints or when space doesn't allow you access to drive screws or nails from behind the joint.

Make sure to buy hot-dipped galvanized or stainless steel connecting hardware.

Tip

Metal connector product labels should identify whether or not the hardware is suitable for pressure-treated wood and outdoor use. Only use hangers rated for exposure to weather and the type of lumber being used. Use joist hanger nails made from the same material as the hardware.

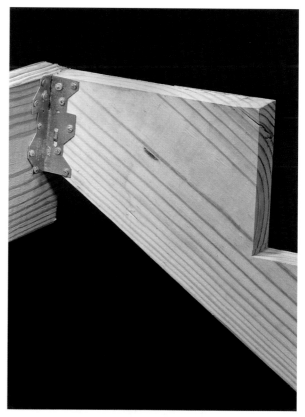

Deck post ties fasten stair or railing posts to stringers or joists without through bolts. Hardware is manufactured in 2 × 4 and 4 × 4 size options.

Framing anchors can be used to fasten rim joists together at corners or make other right-angle attachments, such as stair stringers to rim joists.

Post anchors hold deck posts in place, and raise the base of the posts to help prevent water from entering the end grain of the post.

Angle brackets help reinforce header and outside joists. Angle brackets are also used to attach stair stringers to the deck.

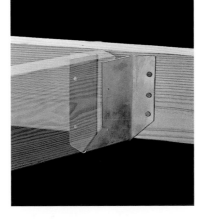

Joist hangers are used to attach joists to the ledger and header joist. Double hangers are used when decking patterns require a double-width joist.

Angled joist hangers are used to frame decks that have unusual angles or decking patterns.

Stair cleats support the treads of deck steps. Cleats are attached to stair stringers with ¼ × 1¼" galvanized lag screws.

Post-beam caps secure beams on top of posts and are available in one-piece or adjustable styles.

H-fit rafter ties attach 2× joists or rafters to the top of a beam between beam ends.

Seismic ties attach 2× joists or rafters to the top of a beam at its ends.

Skewable joist hangers attach 2× lumber, such as stair stringers, to the face of framing at an adjustable angle.

Direct-bearing footing connectors attach beams directly to footings on low profile decks.

Skewable angle brackets reinforce framing connections at angles other than 90° or at beam ends where 45° joist hangers won't fit.

T-straps reinforce the connection between beam and post, particularly on long beams requiring spliced construction. Local building codes may also allow their use in place of post caps.

Strapping plates, also known as nailing plates or mending plates, are useful for a variety of reinforcement applications.

SCREWS & NAILS

When you attach the beams and joists of your deck, and probably the decking as well, you'll need a collection of screws and/or nails to get these jobs done. It may not seem like screw and nail technology would ever change all that much, but in fact there are many new products available for making these essential connections. If you build your deck from pressure-treated lumber, be sure to use stainless, hot-dipped galvanized, or specially coated fasteners that are approved for use with the more corrosive ACQ and CBA wood preservatives. Spiral or ring-shank nails will offer better holding power than smooth nails. Use screws with auger tips and self-drilling heads to avoid drilling pilot holes. Some screws are specially designed for installing composite decking. They have a variable thread pattern that keeps the heads from mushrooming the surrounding material when driven flush.

If you are building a large deck, consider using a pneumatic nailer with collated nails instead of hand nailing. Collated screws are a faster way to lay deck boards than driving each screw individually. Here's an overview of your fastener options.

Tip

Stainless steel screws (left) are expensive, but suitable for all decking materials. Galvanized screws (second from left) are available for treated lumber, and screws with colored coatings (two on right) are formulated to resist corrosion from pressure-treated wood or prevent staining on cedar. Notice that drive choices include square, Phillips, and star. Some deck screws have proprietary drive choices. Make sure you have enough drive bits on hand, as you will be driving many screws.

Use stainless steel or hot-dipped galvanized framing nails to assemble beams and joists. Install metal connector hardware with 8d or 10d hot-dipped galvanized metal connector nails.

For large deck projects, galvanized pneumatic nails or coated, collated screws are a faster way to fasten framing and decking than driving each nail or screw by hand.

If you'd prefer not to see screwheads in your decking but still want to drive them from the surface, you can buy screws with snap-off heads. A special tool breaks the head off after the screw is driven. The resulting hole is much smaller than a screwhead.

Many composite decking manufacturers supply special screw types that hold the material in place better than ordinary screws would, and that are colored to match the decking boards.

Choose your nails and screws carefully. Screws with "bright" or black-oxide coatings and uncoated nails will not stand up to exterior use or pressure-treating chemicals. Fasteners are as crucial to your deck's long-term durability as the quality of the framing lumber or decking.

Make sure your fasteners will resist the corrosive effects of today's pressure-treating chemicals. Fastener manufacturers will usually provide this information on the product label.

FLASHING

Building codes require that a deck's ledger board be attached directly to wall sheathing and house framing, and that a corrosion-resistant flashing material be used at any junction between a deck ledger and a house. If your home is sided, you'll need to remove the siding in the ledger board area before attaching the ledger to the house. Be sure to install 15# or 30# building paper or self-sealing, adhesive backed membrane behind the ledger to prevent moisture damage. Rotting in the area behind the ledger is one of the leading causes of premature deck deterioration. Flashing is particularly important if there's no housewrap behind the siding. Once the ledger is in place, cap it with a piece of galvanized Z-flashing, tucked behind the siding, for added protection.

Building felt, also called building paper, is used behind house siding materials. Use it to replace felt damaged during a ledger installation. Ledger flashing, or Z-flashing, prevents moisture damage behind the deck ledger. Self-sealing membrane provides extra protection from moisture in damp climates or in areas where there is snow accumulation. It can be used over flashing or on top of beams and posts (see below left), and it self-seals around nails or screws that pierce it.

To apply self-sealing membrane, cut a piece to size and position it over the application area. Starting at one end, begin removing the thin plastic backing that protects the adhesive. Firmly press the membrane in place as you remove the backing, working along the installation area. To install long pieces of membrane, enlist the aid of a helper.

Install self-sealing membrane behind the ledger as extra protection from moisture. Apply the membrane over the house wrap or building felt, using the same method shown at left.

FOOTINGS

Footings, which are also called piers, anchor a deck to the ground and create a stable foundation for the posts. They transfer the weight of the deck into the soil and prevent it from heaving upward in climates where the ground freezes. Generally, footings are made from long, hollow tubes of fiber-reinforced paper in several diameters. Once a tube footing is set into the ground below the frostline, you backfill around the outside with soil, tamp it down firmly, and fill with concrete. Metal connective hardware imbedded in the concrete will attach the footings permanently to the deck posts.

Tip

For low-profile platform decks that aren't attached to a house, you may be able to use pre-cast concrete footings instead of buried piers. These footings simply rest on the surface of the soil. Notches on top of the pier are designed to hold joists without fasteners or other hardware.

Lumberyards and building centers will stock round footing forms in various diameters. The diameter you need will depend on the size and weight of your deck. If you are unsure, your building official can help you determine the correct size when you apply for a building permit.

Cut away for clarity

When building heavy decks or placing footings in unstable, loose soil, you may need to use piers with flared footings. Some styles are molded in one piece, or you can attach a flared footing to a conventional footing form with screws.

DECK CONSTRUCTION

REGARDLESS OF THE DECK DESIGN you choose, every permanent deck has a fundamentally similar structure. Posts and footings anchored in the ground, working in tandem with a ledger board fastened to the house, support a framework of beams and joists that form a deck's undercarriage. Decking, railings, and steps are added to this platform to make it accessible and safe. There are proven techniques for installing each of these structural elements, and

that's what you'll learn in this chapter. Once you get comfortable with these skills, you'll be able to apply them to any deck project.

The time it takes to build a deck depends on the size and complexity of the design as well as your building skills. If you're comfortable using tools and start with thorough, accurate plans, you should be able to complete a single-level deck in a few weekends.

A Step-by-Step Overview for Deck Building

DECK-BUILDING IS A PROJECT you'll tackle in stages, no matter what design you choose. Before you begin construction, review the photos on these two pages. They outline the basic procedure you'll want to follow when building your deck. The chapters to follow will explore each of these stages extensively.

Be sure to gather your tools and materials before you begin the project, and arrange to have a helper available for the more difficult stages. Apply for a building permit, where required, and make sure a building inspector has approved the deck design before beginning work.

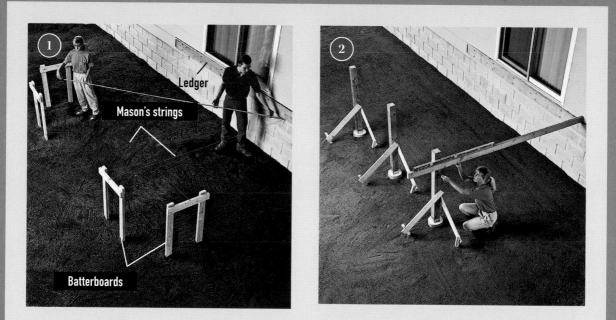

1   Install a ledger to anchor the deck to the house and to serve as reference for laying out footings. Use batterboards and mason's strings to locate footings, and check for square by measuring diagonals.

2   Pour concrete post footings, and install metal post anchors. Set and brace the posts, attach them to the post anchors, and mark posts to show where the beam will be attached.

Tip
Call before you dig! It's required. Call 811 two to three days before you begin digging. Your local utilities will mark the location of underground electrical, telephone, gas, or water lines for you. If you don't call and you damage a line, you may be subject to a fine!

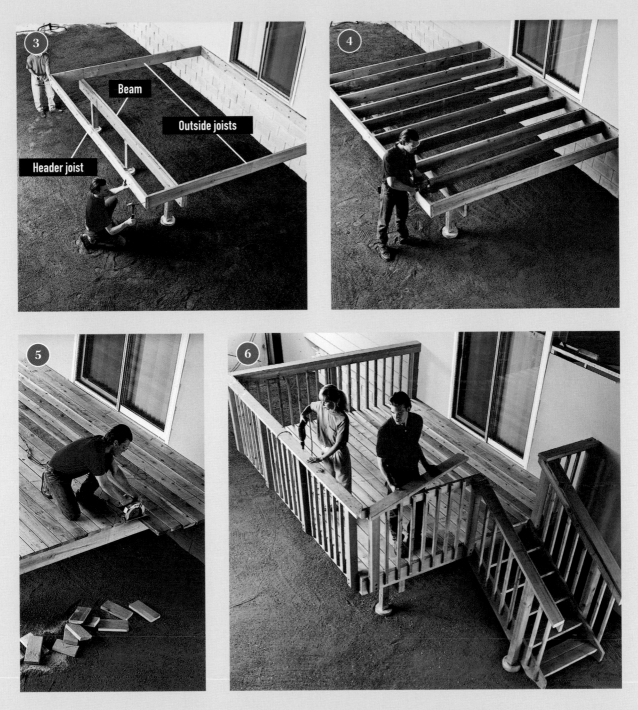

3 Fasten the beam to the posts. Install the outside joists and header joist using galvanized nails.

4 Install metal joist hangers on the ledger and header joist, then hang the remaining joists. Most decking patterns require joists that are spaced 16" on center.

5 Lay decking boards, and trim them with a circular saw. If desired for appearance, cover pressure-treated header and outside joists with redwood or cedar facing boards. Build the deck stairs. Stairs provide access to the deck and establish traffic patterns.

6 Install a railing around the deck and stairway. A railing adds a decorative touch and may be required on any deck that is more than 30" above the ground. If desired, finish the underside of the deck.

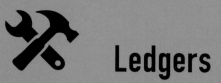

Ledgers

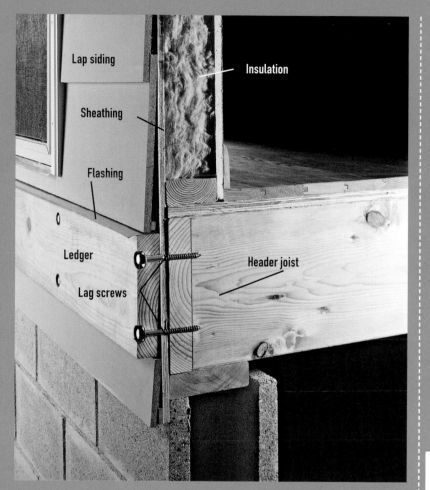

Lap siding

Insulation

Sheathing

Flashing

Ledger

Lag screws

Header joist

Tools & Materials

Pencil
Level
Circular saw with carbide blade
Chisel
Hammer
Metal snips
Caulk gun
Drill and bits
    ($\frac{3}{8}$" twist, $1\frac{3}{8}$" spade,
    $\frac{1}{2}$" and $\frac{5}{8}$–$\frac{3}{4}$" masonry)
Ratchet wrench
Awl
Rubber mallet
Pressure-treated lumber
Galvanized flashing
8d galvanized common nails
Silicone caulk
$\frac{1}{2} \times 4$" lag screws and $1\frac{3}{8}$" washers
Masonry anchors for $\frac{1}{2}$" lag screws
    (for masonry walls)
2×4s for braces

A deck ledger (shown in cross section) is usually made of pressure-treated lumber. Lap siding is cut away to expose sheathing and to provide a flat surface for attaching the ledger. Galvanized flashing tucked under siding prevents moisture damage to wood. Countersunk $\frac{1}{2} \times 4$" lag screws hold the ledger to the header joist inside the house. If there is access to the space behind the header joist, such as in an unfinished basement, attach the ledger with carriage bolts, washers, and nuts.

Tip

Install the ledger so that the surface of the decking boards will be 1" below the indoor floor level. This height difference prevents rainwater or melted snow from seeping into the house.

THE FIRST STEP IN BUILDING an attached deck is to fasten the ledger to the house. The ledger anchors the deck and establishes a reference point for building the deck square and level. The ledger also supports one end of all the deck joists, so it must be attached securely to the framing members of the house.

If your deck's ledger is made from pressure-treated lumber, make sure to use hot-dipped, galvanized lag screws and washers to attach it to the house. Ordinary zinc-coated hardware will corrode and eventually fail if placed in contact with ACQ pressure-treating chemicals. For additional strength on large decks—and where the framing structure will permit it—use through bolts instead of lag screws, tightening down with a washer and nut on the opposite side.

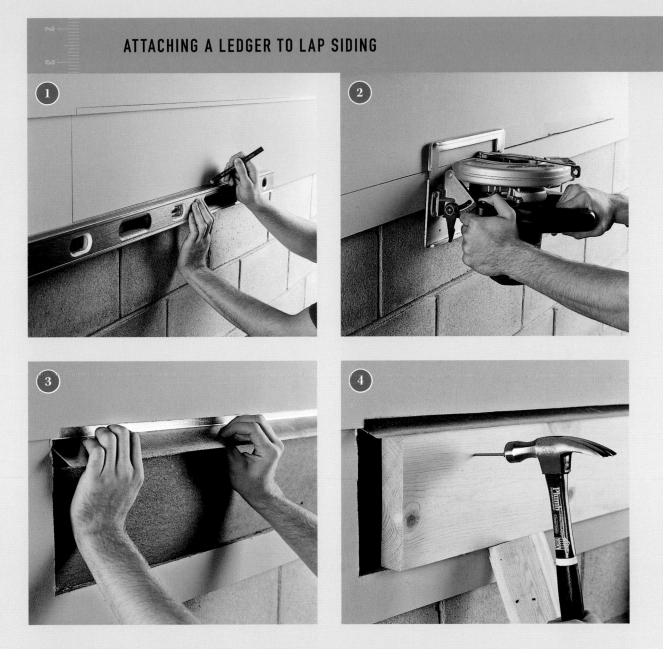

1   Draw an outline showing where the deck will fit against the house, using a level as a guide. Include the thickness of the outside joists and any decorative facing boards that will be installed.

2   Cut out the siding along the outline, using a circular saw. Set the blade depth to the same thickness as the siding, so that the blade does not cut into the sheathing. Use a chisel or oscillating saw to finish the cutout where the circular saw blade does not reach. Hold the chisel with the bevel-side in.

3   Install the self-adhesive moisture barrier and cut galvanized flashing to match the length of the cutout, using metal snips. Slide the flashing up under the siding. Do not nail the flashing in place.

4   Measure and cut the ledger from pressure-treated lumber. Remember that the ledger will be shorter than the overall length of the cutout. Center the ledger in the cutout, underneath the flashing. Brace in position, and tack the ledger into place with 8d galvanized nails. Apply a thick bead of silicone caulk to the space between the siding and flashing.

continued

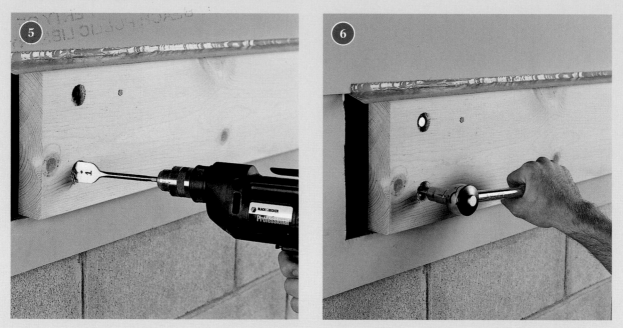

5   Drill pairs of ⅜" pilot holes through the ledger and sheathing, and into the house joist. Space the holes every 2 ft. Counterbore each pilot hole to ½" depth, using a 1⅜" spade bit.

6   Attach the ledger to the wall with ½" × 4" lag screws and washers, using a ratchet wrench or impact driver. Seal lag screw heads with silicone caulk. Seal the crack between the wall and the sides and bottom of the ledger.

Skillbuilder

If you have never used a spade bit to drill a counterbore or used a hammer drill and masonry anchors, it is a good idea to practice first on scrap material.

Clamp a piece of 2× to a work surface. The goal is to drill a hole only ½" deep—any deeper and you compromise the strength of the material. You can buy a portable drill jig for complete accuracy, or you can drill carefully and measure often. Practice drilling and measuring ½" deep holes.

Find a hunk of concrete or concrete block (not a concrete paver) and practice drilling holes with the hammer drill and a masonry bit. Pound masonry anchors into the holes you have drilled and drive lag screws.

ATTACHING A LEDGER TO MASONRY

1   Measure and cut the ledger. The ledger will be shorter than the overall length of the outline. Drill pairs of pilot holes every 2 ft. along the ledger. Counterbore each hole ½" deep, using a 1⅜" spade bit. Draw an outline of the deck on the wall, using a level as a guide. Center the ledger in the outline, and brace in position. Mark the pilot-hole locations on the wall, using an awl or nail. Remove the ledger.

2   Drill anchor holes 3" deep into the wall, using a masonry bit large enough for the anchors.

3   Drive lead masonry anchors for ½" lag screws into the holes, using a rubber mallet.

4   Attach the ledger to the wall with ½ × 4" lag screws and washers, using a ratchet wrench or impact driver. Tighten screws firmly, but do not overtighten.

5   Seal the cracks between the wall and ledger with silicone caulk. Also seal the lag screw heads.

1   Draw the outline of the ledger on the wall, using a level as a guide. Measure and cut the ledger, and drill pilot holes. Brace the ledger against the wall, and mark hole locations using a nail or awl.

2   Remove the ledger. Drill guide holes through the stucco layer of the wall using a ½" masonry bit.

3   Extend each guide hole through the sheathing and into the header joist using a ⅜" bit. Reposition the ledger and brace it in place.

4   Attach the ledger to the wall with ½ × 4" lag screws and washers, using a ratchet wrench or impact driver. Seal the lag screw heads and the cracks between the wall and ledger with silicone caulk.

1   Mark the length of the ledger location, adding 1½"
    at each end to allow for the rim joists that will be
    installed later. Also allow for fascia board thickness
    if it will be added, and create space for metal rim-
    joist hangers. Then mark the top and bottom edges
    of the ledger at both ends of its location. Snap lines
    for the ledger position between the marks. Check
    the lines for level and adjust as necessary. You may
    be able to use the siding edges to help determine the
    ledger location, but only after checking to see if the
    edges are level. Don't assume siding is installed level.

2   Set the circular saw blade depth to cut through the
    siding. Use a metal cutting blade for metal siding; a
    40-tooth carbide blade works well on vinyl siding.
    Cut on the outside of the lines along the top and sides
    of the ledger location, stopping the blade when it
    reaches a corner.

continued

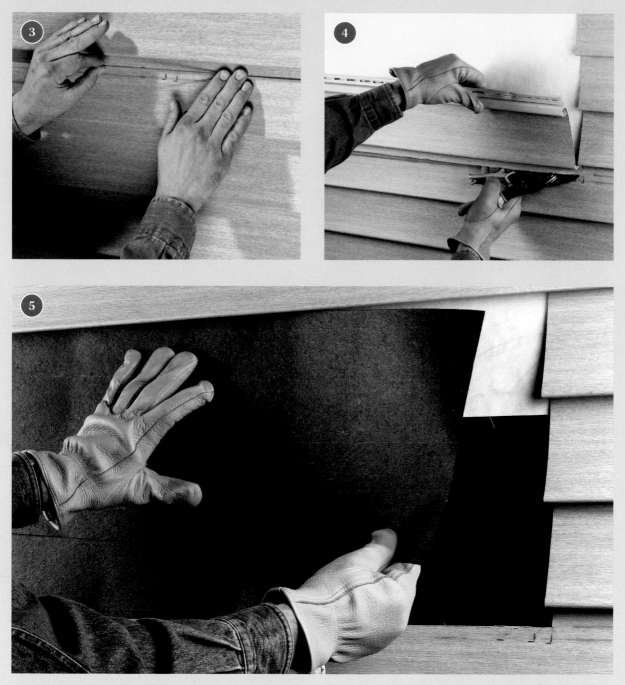

3   Snap a new level line ½" above the bottom line and make your final cut along this line. This leaves a small lip of siding that will fit under the ledger.

4   Complete the cuts in the corners, using tin snips on metal siding or a utility knifc on vinyl siding. An oscillating saw also may be used.

5   Insert building felt underneath the siding and over the existing felt that has been damaged by the cuts. It is easiest to cut and install two long strips. Cut and insert the first strip so it is underneath the siding at the ends and bottom edge of the cutout and attach it with staples. Cut and insert the second strip so it is underneath the siding at the ends and top edge of the cutout, and so that it overlaps the first strip by at least 3".

6   Cut and insert galvanized flashing (also called Z-flashing) underneath the full length of the top edge of the cutout. Do not use fasteners; pressure will hold the flashing in place until the ledger is installed.

7   Cut and install the ledger board. See page 40.

Post Footings

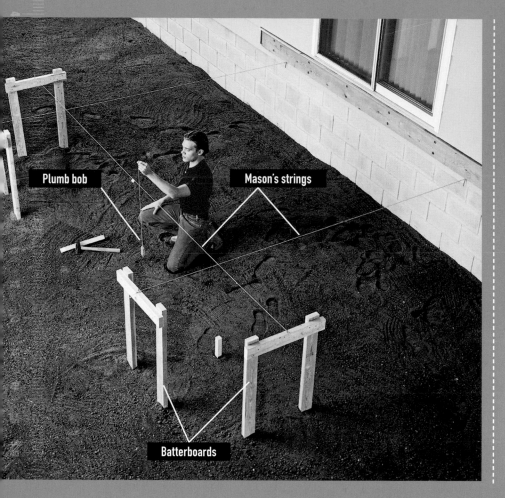

Plumb bob

Mason's strings

Batterboards

Tools & Materials
Tape measure
Felt-tipped pen
Circular saw
Screwgun
Framing square
Masonry hammer
Claw hammer
Line level
Plumb bob
2 × 4s
10d nails
2½" drywall screws
Mason's strings
Masking tape

Tip
You may want to leave the batterboards in place until after the footings are dug. That way, you can use the strings to accurately locate the J-bolts in the concrete.

Mason's strings stretched between the ledger and the batterboards are used to position footings for deck posts. Use a plumb bob and stakes to mark the ground at the exact centerpoints of footings.

ESTABLISH THE EXACT locations of all concrete footings by stretching mason's strings across the site. Use the ledger board as a starting point. These perpendicular layout strings will be used to locate holes for concrete footings and to position metal post anchors on the finished footings. Anchor the layout strings with temporary 2 × 4 supports, often called batterboards.

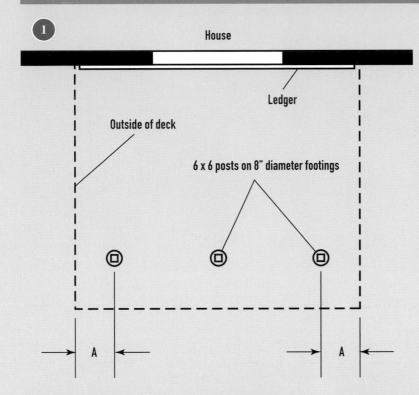

1 Use your design plan to find distance (A). Measure from the side of the deck to the center of each outside post. Use your elevation drawings to find the height of each deck post.

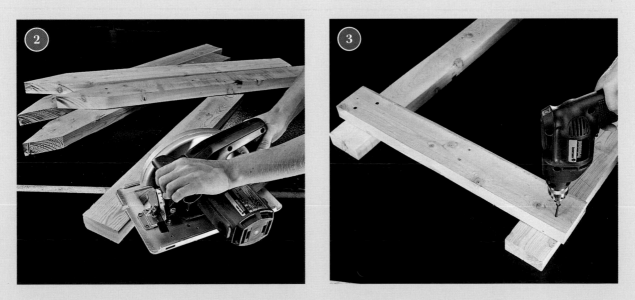

2 Cut 2 × 4 stakes for batterboards, each about 8" longer than post height. Trim one end of each stake to a point, using a circular saw. Cut 2 × 4 crosspieces, each about 2 ft. long.

3 Assemble batterboards by attaching crosspieces to stakes with 2½" wallboard screws. Crosspieces should be about 2" below the tops of the stakes.

continued

4   Transfer measurement A (step 1) to the ledger, and mark reference points at each end of the ledger. String lines will be stretched from these points on the ledger. When measuring, remember to allow for outside joists and facing that will be butted to the ends of the ledger.

5   Drive a batterboard 6" into the ground, about 2 ft. past the post location. The crosspiece of the batterboard should be parallel to the ledger.

6   Drive a 10d nail into the bottom of the ledger at the reference point (step 4). Attach a mason's string to the nail.

7   Extend the mason's string so that it is taut and perpendicular to the ledger. Use a framing square as a guide. Secure the string temporarily by wrapping it several times around the batterboard.

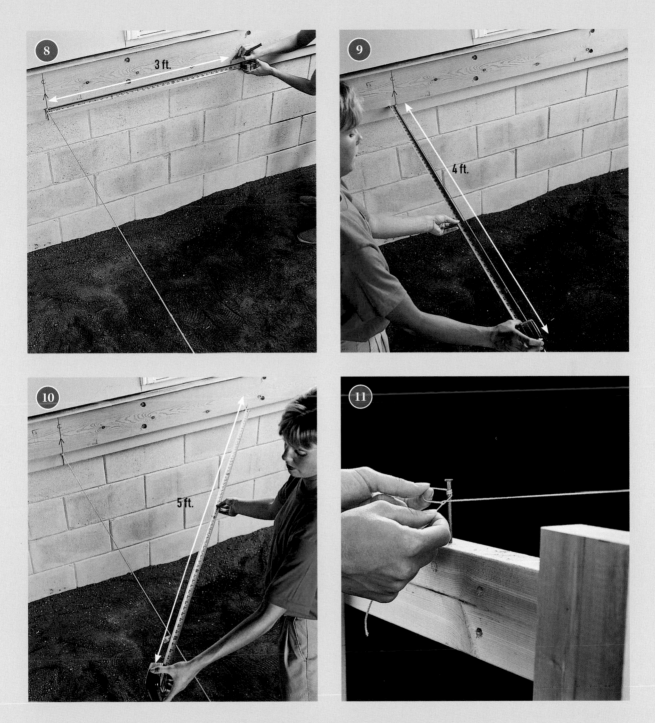

8   Check the mason's string for square using a "3-4-5 carpenter's triangle." First, measure along the ledger 3 ft. from the mason's string and mark a point, using a felt-tipped pen.

9   Measure the mason's string 4 ft. from the edge of the ledger, and mark with masking tape.

10   Measure the distance between the marks. If the string is perpendicular to the ledger, the distance will be exactly 5 ft. If necessary, move the string left or right on the batterboard until the distance between the marks is 5 ft.

11   Drive a 10d nail into the top of the batterboard at the string location. Leave about 2" of nail exposed. Tie the string to the nail.

continued

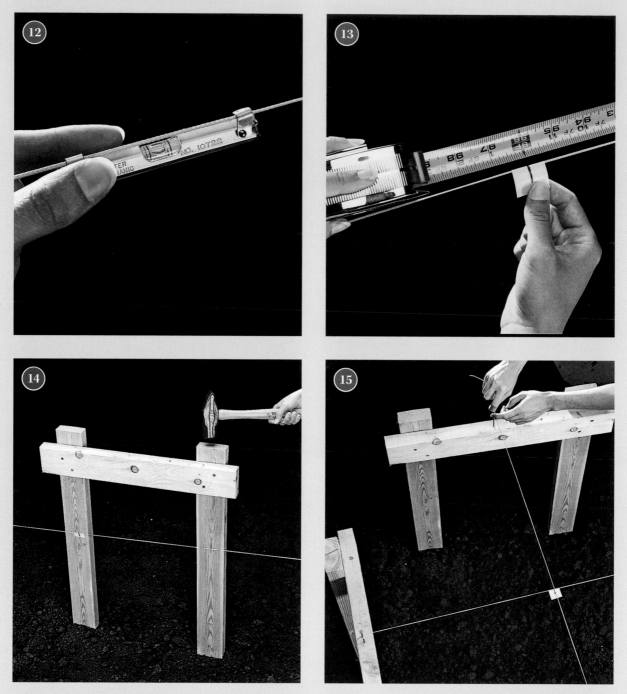

12   Hang a line level on the mason's string. Raise or lower the string until it is level. Locate the other outside post footing, repeating steps 5 to 12.

13   Measure along the mason's strings from the ledger to find the centerpoint of the posts. Mark the centerpoints on the strings, using masking tape.

14   Drive additional batterboards into the ground, about 2 ft. outside of the mason's strings and lined up with the post centerpoint marks (step 13).

15   Align a third cross string with the centerpoint marks on the first strings. Drive 10d nails in new batterboards, and tie off the cross strings on the nails. The cross string should be close to, but not touching, the first strings.

16 Check the strings for square by measuring distances A-B and C-D. Measure the diagonals A-D and B-C from the edge of the ledger to the opposite corners. If the strings are square, measurement A-B will be the same as C-D, and diagonal A-D will be the same as B-C. If necessary, adjust the strings on the batterboards until they are square.

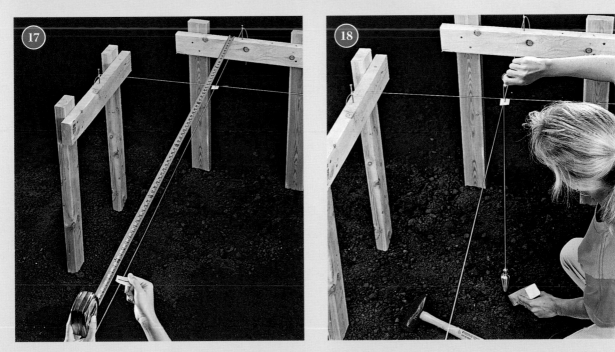

17 Measure along the cross string and mark the centerpoints of any posts that will be installed between the outside posts.

18 Use a plumb bob to mark the post centerpoints on the ground, directly under the marks on the mason's strings. Drive a stake into the ground at each point. Remove the mason's strings before digging the footings.

Footings

CONCRETE FOOTINGS hold deck posts in place and support the weight of the deck. Check local codes to determine the size and depth of footings required for your area. In cold climates, footings must be deeper than the soil frost line.

To help protect posts from water damage, footings are generally poured so that they are at least 2 inches above ground level. You can create footings by pouring concrete directly into a triangular hole with a form on top to create the aboveground portion, or turn to the more common solution of a tube-shaped form that allows you to pour the post you need quickly and easily. Mix your own cement to fill the form by combining Portland cement, sand, gravel, and water. You can also use premixed concrete, which is often a simpler solution.

As an alternative to inserting J-bolts into wet concrete, you can use masonry anchors, metal post brackets with pins, legs, or hooks, or install anchor bolts with an epoxy designed for deck footings and other masonry installations. The epoxy method provides you with more time to reset layout strings for locating bolt locations, and it eliminates the problem of J-bolts tilting or sinking into concrete that is too loose. Most building centers sell threaded rod, washers, nuts, and epoxy syringes, but you can also buy these items separately at most hardware centers.

Before digging, consult local utilities for locations of any underground electrical, telephone, or water lines that might interfere with footings.

Tools & Materials

Power auger or clamshell posthole
    digger
Tape measure
Pruning saw
Shovel
Reciprocating saw or handsaw
Torpedo level
Hoe
Trowel
Shovel
Old toothbrush
Plumb bob
Utility knife
Concrete tube forms
Portland cement
Sand
Gravel
J-bolts
Wheelbarrow
Scrap 2 × 4

Tip

You could dig holes for post footings by hand with a clamshell posthole digger, but a power auger speeds up the task considerably. They are available at rental centers. Some models can be operated by one person, while others require two people. Call before you dig!

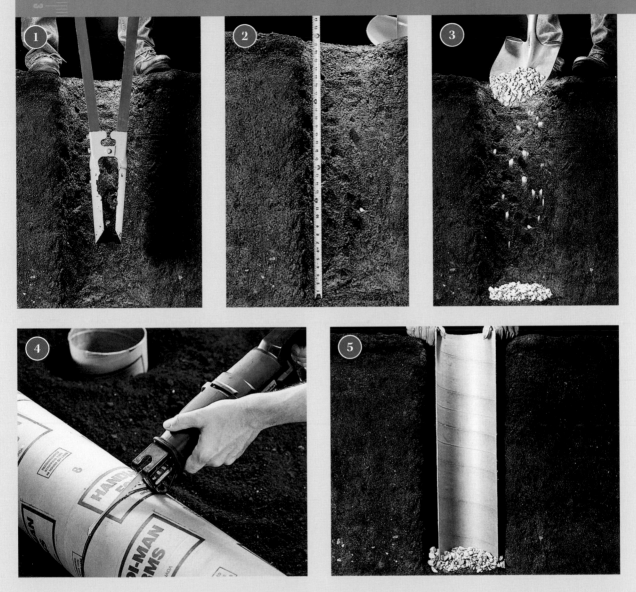

1   Dig holes for post footings with a clamshell digger or power auger, centering the holes on the layout stakes. For holes deeper than 35", use a power auger.

2   Measure hole depth. Local building codes specify depth of footings. Cut away tree roots, if necessary, using a pruning saw.

3   Pour 2" to 3" of loose gravel in the bottom of each footing hole. Gravel will provide drainage under concrete footings.

4   Add 2" to hole depth so that footings will be above ground level. Cut concrete tube forms to length, using a reciprocating saw or handsaw. Make sure the cuts are straight.

5   Insert the tubes into footing holes, leaving about 2" of the tube above ground level. Use a level to make sure the tops of the tubes are level. Pack soil around tubes to hold them in place.

continued

6 Mix the concrete using a basic formula of 4 parts gravel, 2 parts sand to 1 part cement. Mix the dry ingredients with a hoe. Form a hollow in the center of the dry mix, and slowly pour a small amount of water into the hollow. Blend it in using the hoe. Add more water gradually, mixing thoroughly until concrete is firm enough to hold its shape when sliced with a trowel.

7 Pour concrete slowly into the tube form, guiding concrete from the wheelbarrow with a shovel. Fill about half of the form, using a long stick to tamp the concrete, filling any air gaps in the footing. Then finish pouring and tamping concrete into the form.

8 Level the concrete by pulling a 2 × 4 across the top of the tube form, using a sawing motion. Add concrete to any low spots. Retie the mason's strings on the batterboards, and recheck measurements.

9 Insert a J-bolt at an angle into the wet concrete at the center of the footing.

10 Lower the J-bolt slowly into the concrete, wiggling it slightly to eliminate any air gaps.

11 Set the J-bolt so ¾" to 1" is exposed above the concrete. Brush away any wet concrete on the bolt threads with an old toothbrush.

12 Use a plumb bob to make sure the J-bolt is positioned exactly at the center of the post location.

13 Use a torpedo level to make sure the J-bolt is plumb. If necessary, adjust the bolt and repack the concrete. Let the concrete cure, then cut away the exposed portion of tube with a utility knife.

Posts

POSTS SUPPORT the deck beams and transfer the weight of the deck, as well as everything on it, to the concrete footings. They create the above-ground foundation of your deck. Your building inspector will verify that the posts you plan to use are sized correctly to suit your deck design.

Choose post lumber carefully so the posts will be able to carry these substantial loads for the life of your deck. Pressure-treated lumber is your best defense against rot or insect damage. Try not to cut off the factory-treated ends when trimming the posts to length; they contain more of the treatment chemicals and generally last longer than cut ends. Face the factory ends down against the post hardware where water is more likely to accumulate.

Use galvanized metal post anchors to attach the posts to concrete footings. If posts are set directly on concrete, the ends won't dry properly. You'll also have a harder time making the necessary mechanical connection to the footings. Post anchors have drainage holes and pedestals that raise the ends of the wood above the footings and improve drainage. Make sure the posts are installed plumb for maximum strength.

Tools & Materials

Pencil
Framing square
Ratchet wrench
Tape measure
Power miter saw or circular saw
Hammer
Screwgun
Level
Combination square
Metal post anchors
Nuts for J-bolts
Lumber for posts
6d galvanized common nails
2" drywall screws
Long, straight 2 × 4
1 × 4s
Pointed 2 × 2 stakes

Select posts that are straight and free of deep cracks, large knots, or other natural defects that could compromise their strength.

58

ATTACHING POST ANCHORS

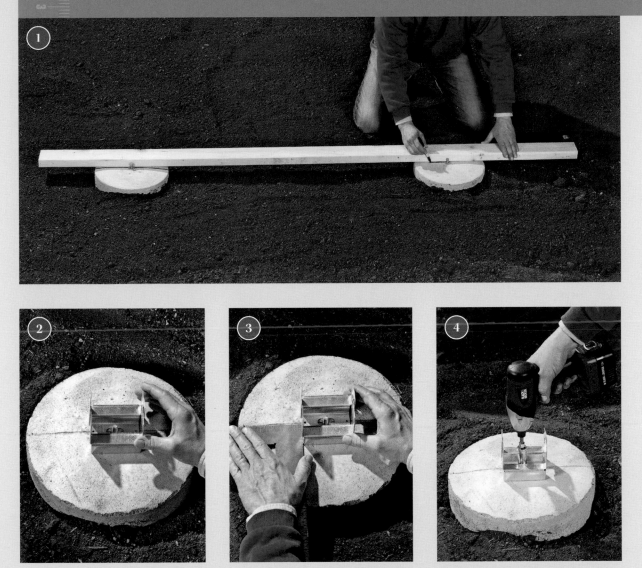

1   Mark the top of each footing as a reference line for installing post anchors. Lay a long, straight 2 × 4 flat across two or three concrete footings, parallel to the ledger, with one edge tight against the J-bolts.

2   Place a metal post anchor on each concrete footing, and center it over the J-bolt.

3   Use a framing square to make sure the post anchor is positioned square to the reference line drawn on the footing.

4   Thread a nut over each J-bolt, and tighten it securely with a ratchet wrench or impact driver.

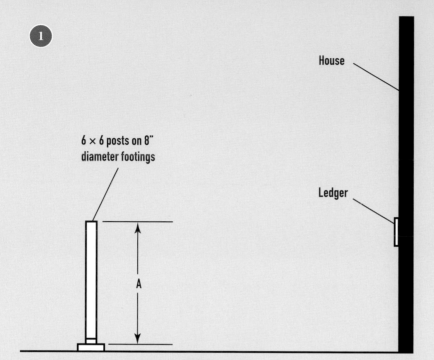

House

**6 × 6 posts on 8"
diameter footings**

Ledger

A

Post elevation

1   Use the elevation drawing from your design plan to find the length of each post (A). Add 6" to the length for a cutting margin.

2   Cut posts to rough length with a power miter saw or circular saw. Make sure factory-treated ends of posts are square. If necessary, square them by trimming with a power miter saw or circular saw.

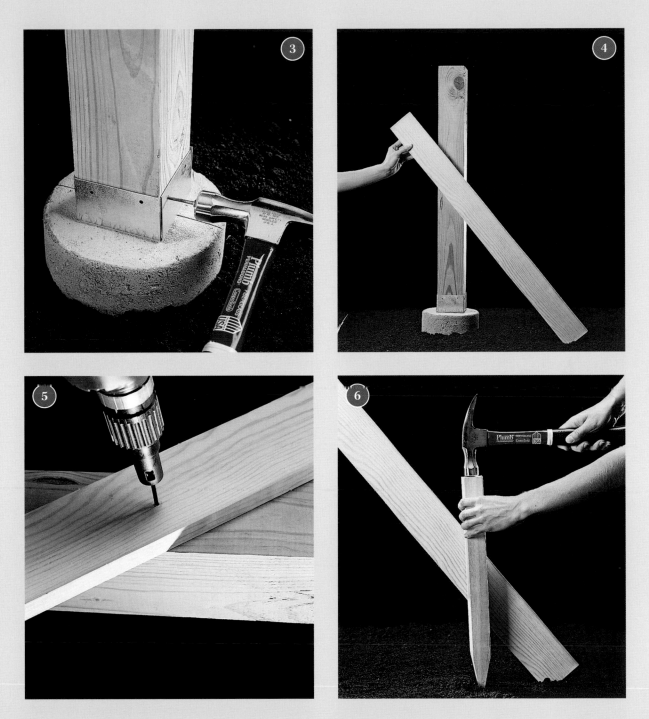

3   Place the post in the anchor and tack it into place with a single 6d galvanized common nail. Do not drive the nail all the way in.

4   Brace the post with a 1 × 4. Place the 1 × 4 flat across the post so that it crosses the post at a 45° angle about halfway up.

5   Attach the brace to the post temporarily with a single 2" drywall or deck screw.

6   Drive a pointed 2 × 2 stake into the ground next to the end of the brace.

continued

7   Use a level to make sure the post is plumb. Adjust the post, if necessary.

8   Attach the brace to the stake with two 2" drywall screws.

9   Plumb and brace the post on the side perpendicular to the first brace.

10 Attach the post to the post anchor with 10d galvanized joist hanger nails. (You can also mark the post, then remove it and cut it on the ground, and then nail it in place.)

11 Position a straight 2 × 4 with one end on the ledger and the other end across the face of the post. Level the 2 × 4. Draw a line on the post along the bottom of the 2 × 4. This line indicates the top of the joists.

12 From the line shown in step 11, measure down and mark the posts a distance equal to the actual width of the joists.

13 Use a square to draw a line completely around the post. This line indicates the top of the beam. From this line, repeat steps 12 and 13 to determine the bottom of the beam.

 # Beams

Tools & Materials

Tape measure
Pencil
Circular saw
Paint brush
Combination square
Screwgun
Drill
½" auger bit
1⅜" spade bit
Ratchet wrench
Caulk gun
Reciprocating saw
    or handsaw
Pressure-treated lumber
Clear sealer-preservative
2½" galvanized deck screws
10d joist hanger nails
½ × 8" carriage bolts with washers
    and nuts
Silicone caulk

Deck beams, resting in a notch on the tops of the posts and secured with through bolts and nuts, guarantee strong connections that will bear the weight of your deck.

DECK BEAMS attach to the posts to help support the weight of the joists and decking. Installation methods depend on the deck design and local codes, so check with a building inspector to determine what is acceptable in your area.

In a saddle beam deck, the beam is attached directly on top of the posts. Metal fasteners, called post-saddles, are used to align and strengthen the beam-to-post connection. The advantage is that the post bears the weight of the deck.

A notched-post deck requires 6 × 6 posts notched at the post top to accommodate the full size of the beam. The deck's weight is transferred to the posts, as in a post-and-beam deck.

Tip

In years past, a third style of beam construction, called sandwiching, was also generally acceptable for deck construction. (You can see an example of it on page 8.) It consisted of two beams that straddled both sides of the post, connected by long through bolts. Because this method has less strength than the saddle or notched styles, it is no longer approved by most building codes.

MARKING POST LOCATIONS ON A BEAM

1 Measure along the beam to the post locations, making sure the ends of the boards of a doubled beam are flush. Mark both the near and far edges of the post onto the beam.

2 Use a combination square or speed square to transfer the post marks onto the top and then the other face of the beam, allowing you to make sure the post and post hardware align with both faces.

FABRICATING A BEAM

1 Select two straight boards of the same dimension (generally 2 × 8 or larger) and lay them face to face to see which alignment comes closest to flush on all sides. Apply exterior grade construction adhesive to one board and lay the mating board onto it. Drive a pair of 10d nails near the end of the assembly to pin the boards together.

2 Clamp the beam members together every 2–3 ft., forcing the boards into alignment as you go, if necessary. Drive 10d nails in a regular, staggered pattern every 12" to 16" or so. Flip the beam over and repeat the nailing pattern from the other side.

1   Cut the post to final height after securing it in place. Make two passes with a circular saw and finish with a reciprocating saw.

2   Attach the saddle hardware to the top of the post using joist hanger screws, 10d galvanized common nails, or joist hanger nails. You must drive a fastener at every predrilled hole in the saddle hardware.

3   Set the beam into the saddle, making sure the sides of the saddle align with the layout marks on the beam.

4   Secure the beam into the saddle by driving galvanized common nails or joist hanger screws through the predrilled holes in the top half of the saddle.

INSTALLING A BEAM FOR A NOTCHED-POST DECK

1   Remove 6 × 6 posts from post anchors and cut to finished height. Measure and mark a notch at the top of each post, sized to fit the thickness and width of the beam. Trace the lines on all sides using a framing square.

2   Use a circular saw to rough-cut the notches, then switch to a reciprocating saw or hand saw to finish. Reattach posts to the post anchors, with the notch-side facing away from the deck.

3   With someone's help, lift the beam (crown side up) into the notches. Align the beam and clamp it to the post. Counterbore two ½"-deep holes, using a 1⅜" spade bit, then drill ½" pilot holes through the beam and post, using a ½" auger bit.

4   Insert carriage bolts to each pilot hole. Add a washer and nut to the counterbore-side of each, and tighten using a ratchet. Seal both ends with silicone caulk. Apply self-sealing membrane to the top surfaces of beam and posts if necessary.

Joists

Tools & Materials

Tape measure
Pencil
Hammer
Combination square
Circular saw
Paintbrush
Drill
Twist bits (⅛", ¼")
Pressure-treated lumber
10d joist hanger nails
10d and 16d galvanized
    common nails
Clear sealer-preservative
Joist angle brackets
Galvanized metal joist hangers

Metal joist hangers attached to rim joists or ledgers are practically foolproof for hanging intermediate deck joists. Look for hanger hardware that is triple-dipped galvanized metal.

JOISTS PROVIDE SUPPORT for the decking boards. They are attached to the ledger and header joist with galvanized metal joist hangers and are nailed or strapped to the top of the beam. For strength and durability, use pressure-treated lumber for all joists.

Tip

Trim off the ends of structural lumber to get a clean, straight edge.

Tip

The exposed outside joists and header joist can be faced with composite or cedar boards for a more attractive appearance.

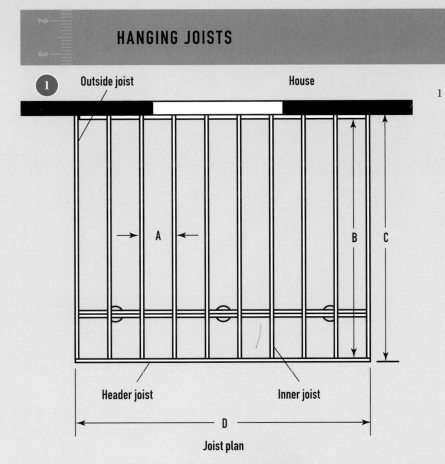

1 Outside joist   House

A

B   C

Header joist   Inner joist

D

Joist plan

1 Use your deck plan to find the spacing (A) between joists, and the length of inner joists (B), outside joists (C), and the header joist (D). Measure and mark lumber for outside joists using a combination square as a guide. Cut joists with a miter or circular saw. Seal cut ends with clear sealer-preservative.

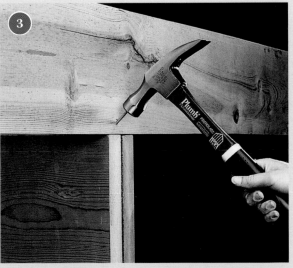

2 Attach joist hanger hardware near each end of the ledger board, according to your layout. Previous building codes allowed you to face nail the joists into the ends of the ledger, but this is no longer accepted practice. Attach only enough fasteners to hold the hanger in position while you square up the joist layout.

3 Attach the outside joists to the top of the beam by toenailing them with 10d galvanized common nails.

continued

4   Measure and cut the header joist. Seal cut ends with clear sealer-preservative. Drill ⅛" pilot holes at each end of the header joist. Attach the header to ends of outside joists with 16d galvanized common nails. For extra reinforcement, add metal corner brackets to the inside corner joints.

Outside joist

Ledger

Beam

Header joist

Outside joist

5   Finish nailing the end joist hangers, making sure you have a joist hanger nail in every punched hole in the hanger.

6   Measure along the ledger from the edge of the outside joist, and mark where the joists will be attached to the ledger. Draw the outline of each joist on the ledger, using a square as a guide.

7   Measure along the beam from the outside joist, and mark where joists will cross the beam. Draw the outlines across the top of both beam boards.

8   Measure along the header joist from the outside joist, and mark where joists will be attached to the header joist. Draw the outlines on the inside of the header, using a square as a guide.

9   Attach joist hangers to the ledger and to the header joist. Position each hanger so that one of the flanges is against the joist outline. Nail one flange to framing members with 10d galvanized joist hanger nails.

10 Cut a scrap board to use as a spacer. Hold the spacer inside each joist hanger, then close the hanger around the spacer.

continued

11 Nail the remaining side flange to the framing member with 10d joist hanger nails. Remove the spacer. Measure and mark lumber for joists, using a combination square as a guide. Cut joists with a circular saw or power miter saw.

12 Seal cut ends with clear sealer-preservative. Place the joists in the hangers with crowned edge up.

13 Attach the ledger joist hangers to the joists with joist hanger nails. Drive nails into both sides of each joist.

14 Align the joists with the outlines drawn on the top of the beam. Anchor the joists to the beam by toenailing from both sides with 10d galvanized nails.

15 Attach the joists to the hangers on the joist with 10d joist hanger nails. Drive nails into both sides of each joist.

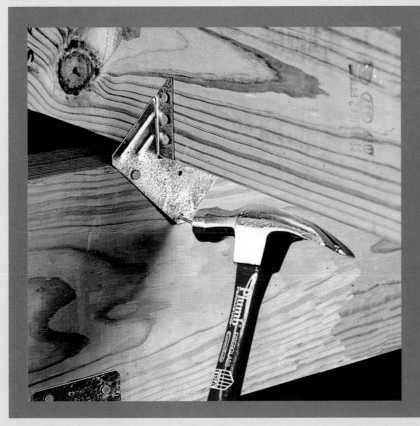

Alternate Method

Fasten joists to beams using H-fit joist ties for strength and durability.

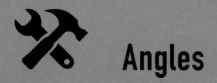

Angles

Joists on a cantilevered deck can be easily marked for angled cuts by snapping a chalk line between two points on adjacent sides of the deck corner. Marking and cutting joists in this fashion is easier than measuring and cutting the joists individually. To help hold the joists in place while marking, tack a brace across the ends. Mark joist locations on the brace for reference.

DECKS WITH GEOMETRIC SHAPES and angled sides have much more visual interest than basic square or rectangular decks. Most homes and yards are configured with predictable 90-degree angles and straight sides, so an angled deck offers a pleasing visual surprise.

Contrary to popular belief, elaborate angled decks are relatively easy to plan and build, if you follow the lead of professional designers. As professionals know, most polygon-shaped decks are nothing more than basic square or rectangular shapes with one or more corners removed.

Seen in this light, complicated multi-level decks with many sides become easier to visualize and design.

For visual balance and ease of construction, use 45-degree angles when designing an angled, geometric deck. In this way, the joinery requires only common cutting angles (90-degree, 45-degree, or 22½-degree), and you can use skewed 45-degree joist hangers, readily available at home centers. The angled deck construction shown on the following pages was built using primarily 4 × 4 inch posts. Recent changes to many building codes require 6 × 6 inch posts. Always check with your local building department to learn applicable codes for your deck.

Cantilever design is the easiest and least expensive to build, since it requires the fewest posts. But the length of the angled side is limited by code regulations that restrict the amount of joist overhang. And since the joists rest on top of the beam, cantilever designs are not suited for a deck with a very low profile. On cantilever designs, the joists along the angled side are beveled at 45° at the ends, and are attached to the rim joist by endnailing.

Corner-post design is a good choice for large decks with long, angled sides. It also works well for low-profile decks, since the joists are mounted to the inside faces of the beams. Many builders use a single beveled post to support the angled corners on this type of deck, but our method calls for two posts and footings at each of these corners, making the design easier to construct and more versatile. On a corner-post deck, the joists on the angled side are square-cut, and are attached to the beam with skewed 45° joist hangers.

Multi-level design features an upper platform built using the corner-post method (above), but adds a lower platform. The lower level is supported by a second angled beam, created by sandwiching timbers around the same posts that support the upper platform. On the lower platform, the joists rest on top of the beam and are beveled on the back ends so they are flush with the edge of the beam. Check with your local building department to make sure this design strategy is allowed by your local building codes.

Tip

An octagonal island deck is simply a square with all four corners omitted.

1. Lay out and begin construction, using standard deck-building techniques. After installing the joists, mark cutting lines on the angled side by snapping a chalk line across the tops of the joists. Make sure the chalk line is angled 45° to the edge of the deck.

2. At the outside joists, use a speed square to change the 45° chalk line to a line angled at 22½° in the opposite direction. When joined to a rim joist that is also cut to 22½°, the corner will form the correct angle.

3. Use a combination square to extend the angle marks down the faces of the joists. Bevel-cut the deck joists with a circular saw, using a clamped board as a guide for the saw foot. Interior joists should be beveled to 45°; outside joists to 22½°.

4. Cut and install the rim joists. At the angled corners, bevel-cut the ends of the rim joists at 22½°. Endnail the rim joists in place, and reinforce the inside corners with adjustable angle brackets attached with joist-hanger nails. Finish the deck using standard deck-building techniques.

1   Use boards to create a rectangular template of the deck. To ensure that the template is square, use the 3-4-5 triangle method: From the corner directly below the ledger, measure 3 ft. along the foundation, and mark a point. Measure out along the template board 4 ft., and mark a second point. Measure diagonally between the two points. This measurement should be 5 ft.; if not, adjust the template to square it.

2   Indicate each angled edge by positioning a board diagonally across the corner of the template. To ensure that the angles measure 45°, make sure the perpendicular legs of the triangle have exactly the same measurement. Nail the boards together where they overlap.

3   Mark locations for post footings with stakes or spray paint. At each 45° corner, mark locations for two posts, positioned about 1 ft. on each side of the corner. Temporarily move the board template, then dig and pour concrete footings.

4   While the concrete is still wet, reposition the template and check to make sure it is square to the ledger. Use a nail to scratch a reference line across the concrete next to the template boards, then insert J-bolts in the wet concrete. Let the concrete dry completely.

continued

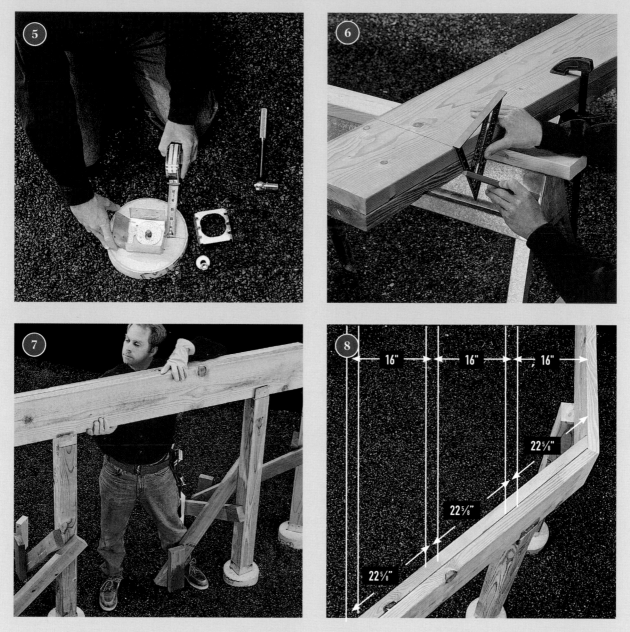

5 Attach metal post anchors to the J-bolts, centering them on the reference lines scratched in the concrete. The front and back edges of the anchors should be parallel to the reference line.

6 Measure and cut beam timbers to size. On ends that will form angled corners, use a speed square to mark 22½° angles on the tops of the timbers, then use a combination square to extend cutting lines down the face of the boards. Use a circular saw set for a 22½° bevel to cut off the timbers, then join them together with 16d nails.

7 Set posts into the post anchors, then use a mason's string and line level to mark cutoff lines on the posts at a point level with the bottom of the ledger. Cut off the posts using a circular saw. Attach post-beam caps to the posts, then set the beams into place. Secure beam corners together with adjustable angle brackets attached to the inside of each corner with joist-hanger nails.

8 Measure and mark joist locations on the ledger and beams. If your joists are spaced 16" on center along the ledger, they will be spaced 22⅝" apart measured along the angled beam. If they are spaced 24" on center at the ledger, the joists will be spaced 33⁵⁄₁₆" apart along the angled beam.

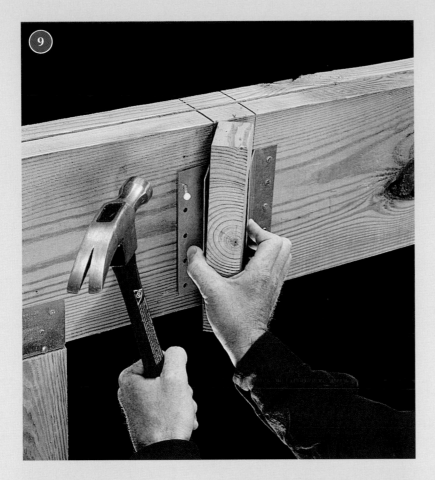

9   Attach joist hangers at the layout marks on the ledger and beam. Use skewed 45° joist hangers on the angled beam.

10 Cut and install joists, securing them with joist-hanger nails. Joists installed in skewed 45° joist hangers can be square-cut; they need not be beveled to match the angle of the beam. Complete the deck, using standard deck-building techniques.

Curves

BY THEIR NATURE, curved shapes lend a feeling of tranquility to a landscape. A deck with curved sides tends to encourage quiet relaxation. A curved deck can also provide an effective visual transition between the sharp architectural angles of the house and the more sweeping natural lines of the surrounding landscape.

Curved decks nearly always use a cantilevered design, in which the curved portion of the deck overhangs a beam that is set back from the edge of the deck. This setback distance generally should be no more than one-third of the total length of the deck joists, but longer cantilevers are possible if you use a combination of thicker joists, closer joist spacing, and stronger wood species, such as southern yellow pine.

The curved deck shown on the following pages was built using primarily 4 × 4 inch posts. Recent changes to many building codes require 6 × 6 inch posts. Always check with your local building department to learn applicable codes for your deck.

If your curved deck will be high enough to require a railing, we recommend a design that incorporates a circular curve rather than an elliptical or irregular curve. Adding a curved railing is much easier if the deck curve is based on a circular shape.

Tip

Adding curves to your deck is not something you should do on the spur of the moment. Consider the pros and cons carefully before you commit to curves. Here are some to think about:

Pros:
- Curves can add visual appeal and uniqueness to your deck.
- Curves soften the overall feeling.
- Used wisely, curves have a natural, organic visual quality.
- A curve can be used to work around an obstacle in a pleasing way.
- A curved corner can preserve space below the deck.

Cons:
- Decks that incorporate curves almost always require more posts and beams, and they make less efficient use of building materials.
- A deck with curves takes at least twice as long to build as a square or rectangular one.
- Curved railings are tricky to make.
- Impact is lessened if curves are overused.
- Curves reduce and constrict deck floorspace.

A curved deck is created by cutting joists to match the curved profile, then attaching a curved rim joist, which can be shaped in one of two ways (page opposite). Braces attached to the tops of the joists hold them in place as the rim joist is installed.

DESIGN OPTIONS FOR CURVED DECKS

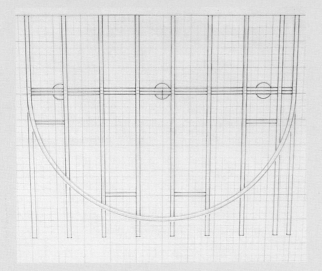

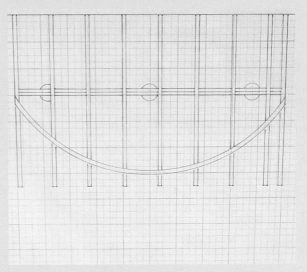

Circular designs are the best choice for curved decks that require railings. However, circular curves require a fairly long cantilever, a limitation that may limit the overall size of your deck. Circular decks are laid out using simple geometry and a long compass tool, called a trammel, which you can make yourself.

Irregular or elliptical curves should be used only on relatively low decks, since railings are quite difficult to construct for this kind of curve. These designs also work well for large decks, since the amount of overhang on the cantilever is relatively short compared to that for a circular curve.

CONSTRUCTION OPTIONS FOR CURVES

A kerfed rim joist is formed by making a series of thin vertical cuts (kerfs) across the inside face of the board, making it flexible enough to wrap around the curve. A kerfed rim joist made from 2"-thick dimension lumber is sufficiently strong, but if you are kerfing a 1"-thick redwood or cedar fascia board, it should be backed with a laminated rim joist (photo, right).

Laminated rim joist is made by bending several layers of flexible ¼"- or ⅜"-thick exterior-grade plywood around the curve, joining each layer to the preceding layer with glue and screws. A laminated rim joist can stand alone, or it can provide backing for a more decorative fascia, such as a kerfed redwood or cedar board.

1   Install posts and beam for a cantilevered deck. Cut joists slightly longer than their final length, and attach them to the ledger and the beam. Add cross-blocking between the two outside joists to ensure that they remain plumb.

2   Mark the joist spacing on a 1 × 4 brace, and tack it across the tops of the joists at the point where the deck curve will begin. Measure the distance between the inside edges of the outer joists at each end of the beam, then divide this measurement in half to determine the radius of the circular curve. Mark the 1 × 4 brace to indicate the midpoint of the curve.

3   Build a trammel by anchoring one end of a long, straight 1 × 2 to the centerpoint of the curve, using a nail. (If the centerpoint lies between joists, attach a 1 × 4 brace across the joists to provide an anchor.) Measure out along the arm of the trammel a distance equal to the curve radius, and drill a hole. Insert a pencil in the hole, and pivot the trammel around the centerpoint, marking the joists for angled cuts.

Variation

For elliptical or irregular curves, temporarily nail vertical anchor boards to the outside joists at the start of the curve. Position a long strip of flexible material, such as hardboard or paneling, inside the anchor boards, then push the strip to create the desired bow. Drive nails into the joists to hold the bow in position, then scribe cutting lines on the tops of the joists.

4 Use a speed square or protractor to determine the bevel angles you will use to cut the joists. Position the square so the top is aligned with the layout mark on the joist, then find the degree measurement by following the edge of the joist down from the pivot point and reading where it intersects the degree scale on the square.

5 Use a combination square to extend the cutting lines down the front and back faces of the joists. At the outside joists where the curve begins, mark square cutting lines at the point where the circular curve touches the inside edge of the joists.

6 Cut off each joist with a circular saw set to the proper bevel. Clamp a straightedge to the joist to provide a guide for the foot of the saw. On the outside joists where the curve begins, make 90° cuts.

7 Where the bevel angle is beyond the range of your circular saw, use a reciprocating saw to cut off the joists.

CONSTRUCTING A KERFED RIM JOIST FOR A CURVED DECK

Blocking

Additional cross block

1   Mark the inside face of the rim joist lumber with a series of parallel lines, 1" apart. Using a circular saw or radial-arm saw set to a blade depth equal to ¾ of the rim joist thickness (1⅛" for 1½"-thick lumber), make crosscut kerfs at each line. Soak the rim joist in hot water for about 2 hours to make it easier to bend.

2   Install a cross block between the first two joists on each side of the curve, positioned so half the block is covered by the square-cut outside joist (inset). While it is still damp, attach the rim joist by butting it against the end joist and attaching it to the cross block with 3" deck screws. Bend the rim joist so it is flush against the ends of the joists, and attach with two or three 3" deck screws driven at each joist.

3   Where butt joints are necessary, mark and cut the rim joist so the joint will fall at the center of a joist. To avoid chipping, cut off the rim joist at one of the saw kerfs.

4   Complete the installation by butting the end of the rim joist against the outside joist and attaching it to the cross block. Use bar clamps to hold the rim joist in position as you screw it to the blocking. If the rim joist flattens near the sides of the deck, install additional cross-blocking, cut to the contour of the curve, to hold the rim joist in proper position.

CONSTRUCTING A CURVED RIM JOIST WITH LAMINATED PLYWOOD

1   Install blocking between the first two joists on each side of the deck (step 2, previous page). Cut four strips of
    ¼"-thick exterior plywood the same width as the joists. Butt the first strip against the outside joist and attach it
    to the blocking with 1⅝" deck screws. Bend the strip around the joists and attach with deck screws. If necessary,
    install additional blocking to keep the plywood in the proper curve. If butt joints are necessary, make sure they fall
    at the centers of joists.

2   Attach the remaining strips of plywood one at a time, attaching them to previous layers with 1" deck screws and
    exterior wood glue. Make sure butt joints are staggered so they do not overlap previous joints. For the last layer, use
    a finish strip of ⅜" cedar plywood. Where the finish strip butts against the outside joists, bevel-cut the ends at 10° to
    ensure a tight fit.

INSTALLING DECKING ON A CURVED DECK

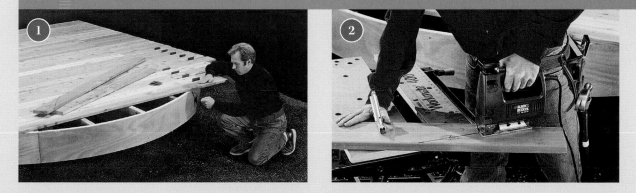

1   Install decking for the square portion of the deck, then test-fit decking boards on the curved portion. If necessary,
    you can make minor adjustments in the spacing to avoid cutting very narrow decking boards at the end of the
    curve. When satisfied with the layout, scribe cutting lines on the underside of the decking boards, following the
    edge of the rim joist.

2   Remove the scribed decking boards, and cut along the cutting lines with a jig saw. Install the decking boards
    with deck screws, and smooth the cut edges of the decking boards with a belt sander or random-orbit sander,
    if necessary.

Insets

IF YOUR PLANNED deck site has a tree, boulder, or other large obstacle, you may be better off building around it rather than removing it. Although framing around a landscape feature makes construction more difficult, the benefits usually make the effort worthwhile. A deck with an attractive tree set into it, for example, is much more appealing than a stark, exposed deck built on a site that has been leveled by a bulldozer.

The same methods used to frame around a preexisting obstacle also can be used to create a decorative or functional inset feature, such as a planter box, child's sandbox, or brick barbecue. On a larger scale, the same framing techniques can be used to enclose a hot tub or above-ground pool.

Tip

A framed opening can also provide access to a utility fixture, such as a water faucet, electrical outlet, or central air-conditioning compressor. Covering a framed opening with a removable hatch preserves the smooth, finished look of your deck.

Inset framing makes it possible to save mature trees when building a deck. Keeping trees and other landscape features intact helps preserve the value and appearance of your property. Check with a tree nursery for an adequate opening size for any tree you want to contain within an inset.

Large insets that interrupt joists can compromise the strength of your deck. For this reason, inset openings require modified framing to ensure adequate strength. Double joists on either side of the opening bear the weight of double headers, which in turn support the interrupted joists. Always consult your building inspector for specifics when constructing a deck with a large inset.

1   Modify your deck plan, if necessary, to provide the proper support for the interrupted joists in the inset opening. If the inset will interrupt one or two joists, frame both sides of the opening with double joists. If the opening is larger, you may need to install additional beams and posts around the opening to provide adequate support. Consult your building inspector for specific requirements for your situation.

2   Rough-frame the opening by using double joist hangers to install double joists on each side of the inset, and double headers between these joists. Install the interrupted joists between the double headers and the rim joist and ledger.

3   Where needed, cut and install angled nailing blocks between the joists and headers to provide additional support for the decking boards. When trimmed, decking boards may overhang support members by as much as 4" around an inset opening.

FINISHING DECKS

JUST LIKE CLOTHES MAKE THE MAN, design details make the deck. Although there's no crime in building a simple, plan platform to take advantage of a backyard view, or as a no-frills summer hangout to share a few drinks with friends, it's the very rare deck that isn't improved with one or more built-in features.

Some of these are required. Handrails, for instance, are mandated by local codes for decks a certain height above the ground. Stairs are simply practical necessities for elevated or multilevel decks. As practical as these features may be, however, they can also be built with incredible style.

DECKING PATTERNS

Decking boards are the most visible element of your deck, and there are a number of ways to install them. You can use different board widths and lay the boards in any of a number of patterns to increase visual interest. The pattern you choose will affect joist spacing and layout. For instance, a straight decking pattern usually requires joists spaced 16 inches on-center. Diagonal decking generally requires joist spacing of 12 inches on-center. Parquet and other intricate patterns may require extra support, such as double joists or additional blocking. For sturdy wood decking, always use at least 5/4 lumber. Thinner boards are more likely to twist or cup.

Diagonal decking is one of the simplest alternatives to straight runs, and can be an interesting look—especially if you run the diagonals in different directions on different platforms or levels of the deck. However, diagonal patterns often require joists spaced closer than a straight pattern.

Parquet patterns are visually stunning and best suited to more formal decks, and those that don't include bi- or multicolored design features. These patterns require double joists and blocking to provide adequate support surface for attaching the butted ends of boards.

Even a straight pattern can be interesting when interrupted with built-in shapes. A framed opening for a tree or large rock requires extra blocking between joists. Short joists are attached to blocking with joist hangers.

Border patterns with mitered corners provide an elegant finished look to any deck. They are especially effective when used around the inside deck edge bordering a swimming pool. Install trim joists to support the border decking.

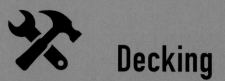

Decking

BUY DECKING BOARDS that are long enough to span the width of the deck, if possible. If you have to use more than one, butt the boards end-to-end over a joist. Install decking so that there is a gap approximately ⅛" between boards to provide drainage. You can use a nail as a spacer between rows. Some wood boards naturally "cup" as they age. Lay the boards with the bark side facing down, so that any cupping occurs on the bottom side, and to prevent the board holding water on the top.

The common installation method for wood decking is shown here. We've limited the discussion to face-screwing boards to joists, but you can nail the boards down as well. However, nailing is rarely used on modern decking because it requires as much work, and nails inevitably pop up. Screws are just more efficient. If you do decide to nail boards down, use 10d galvanized common nails, angling the nails toward each other to improve holding power. Composite and plastic deck boards are never nailed down. For a much sleeker appearance, you can choose from the large number of "invisible" fasteners on the market. The technology for these has come a long way and, whether you're using wood, composite, or another type of deck boards, hidden fasteners are an easy, quick, and just a slightly more expensive option than screwing the boards down. In any case, always follow the installation instructions and methods recommended by the manufacturer of the product you select.

Tools & Materials

Tape measure
Circular saw
Screwgun
Hammer
Drill
⅛" twist bit
Pry bar
Chalk line
Jigsaw or handsaw
Decking boards
2½" corrosion-resistant deck screws
Galvanized common nails (8d, 10d)
Redwood or cedar facing boards

Tip

Stagger butted joints so that they do not overlap row to row.

Tip: Using a Template

Lay the decking boards so the ends overhang the rough opening. Make a cardboard template to draw a cutting line on the deck boards. (When framing for a tree, check with a tree nursery for adequate opening size to provide space for growth.) Cut the decking boards along the marked line, using a jigsaw. Unattached deckboards can also be cut to curved profiles with a jigsaw.

Skillbuilder

Driving fasteners through damp treated lumber requires a powerful drill/driver. Before beginning your construction project, try driving fasteners into scraps of treated lumber. You may find that your cordless drill/driver does not have the oomph to drive hundreds of fasteners into the dense treated lumber. Upgrade to a higher voltage tool, or drag out the adjustable speed corded drill and use it as a driver. Because corded drills don't have a clutch, you will need to dial down the speed and take care not to strip out the screws.

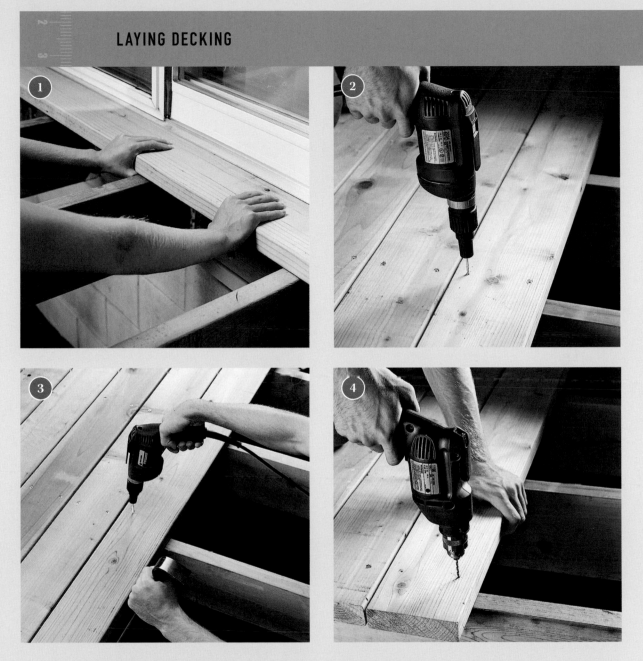

1. Position the first row of decking flush against the house. The first decking board should be perfectly straight, and should be precut to proper length. Attach the first decking board by driving a pair of 2½" corrosion-resistant deck screws into each joist.

2. Position remaining decking boards so that ends overhang outside joists. Space boards about ⅛" apart. Attach boards to each joist with a pair of 2½" deck screws driven into each joist.

3. If the boards are bowed, use a pry bar to maneuver them into position while fastening. You can also use a specialized tool to align a warped board.

4. Drill ⅛" pilot holes in the ends of boards before attaching them to the outside joists. Pilot holes prevent screws from splitting decking boards at ends.

continued

Tip

Adjust board spacing by changing the gaps between boards by a small amount over three or four rows of boards. Very small spacing changes will not be obvious to the eye.

5   After every few rows of decking are installed, measure from the edge of the decking board to the edge of header joist. If the measurements show that the last board will not fit flush against the edge of the deck, adjust board spacing.

6   Use a chalk line to mark the edge of the decking flush with the outside of deck. Cut off decking, using a circular saw. Set the saw blade ⅛" deeper than the thickness of the decking so that the saw will not cut the side of the deck. At areas where the circular saw cannot reach, finish the cutoff with a jigsaw or handsaw.

7   For a more attractive appearance, face the deck with redwood or cedar facing boards. Miter cut corners, and attach boards with deck screws or 8d galvanized nails.

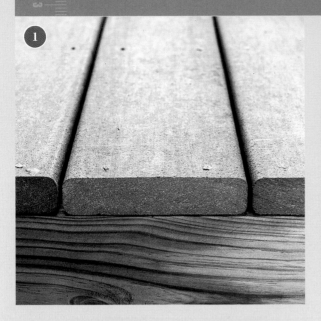

1   Lay composite decking as you would wood decking (previous pages). Position with the factory crown up so water will run off, and space rows ⅛" to ¼" apart for drainage.

2   Predrill pilot holes at ¾ the diameter of the fasteners, but do not countersink. Composite materials allow fasteners to set themselves. Use spiral shank nails, hot-dipped galvanized ceramic coated screws, or stainless steel nails or deck screws.

3   Lay remaining decking. For boards 16 ft. or shorter, leave a gap at deck ends and any butt joints, ¹⁄₁₆" for every 20°F difference between the temperature at the time of installation and the expected high temperature for the year.

Cutaway for clarity

Alternate method:

Attach composite decking with self-tapping composite screws. These specially designed screws require no pilot holes. If the decking "mushrooms" over the screw head, use a hammer to tap back in place.

LAYING TONGUE-AND-GROOVE DECKING

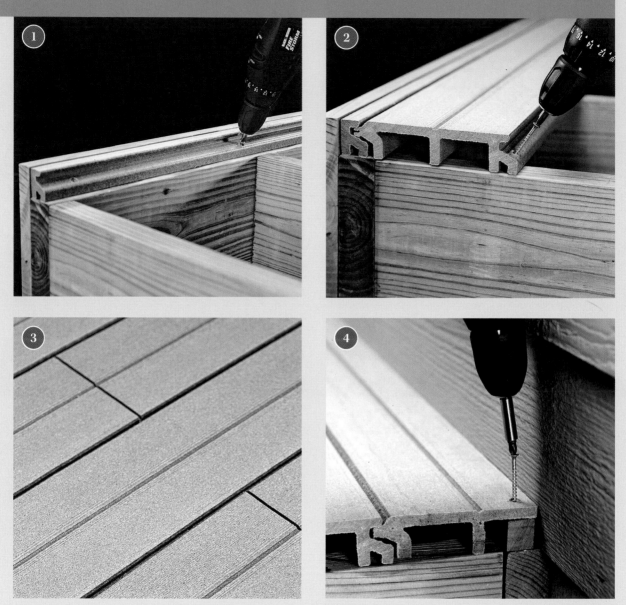

1   Position the starter strip at the far end of the deck. Make sure it is straight and properly aligned. Attach it with 2½" galvanized deck screws driven into the lower runner found under the lip of the starter strip.

2   Fit the tongue of a deck board into the groove of the starter strip. There will be approximately a ¼" gap between the deck board and the starter strip. Fasten the deck board to the joists with 2½" galvanized deck screws, working from the middle out to the sides of the deck.

3   Continue to add decking. To lay deck boards end-to-end, leave a ⅛" gap between them, and make sure any butt joints are centered over a joist.

4   Place the final deck board and attach it with 2½" galvanized deck screws driven through the top of the deck board into the joist. If necessary, rip the final board to size, then support the board with a length of 1 × 1 and attach both to the joist. Attach facing boards to conceal exposed ends (photo 4, next page).

1   Insert 2" galvanized deck screws into T-clips. Loosely attach one T-clip to the ledger at each joist location.

2   Position a deck board tight against the T-clips. Loosely attach T-clips against bottom lip on front side of deck board, just tight enough to keep the board in place. Fully tighten T-clips at the back of the board, against the house.

3   Push another deck board tightly against the front T-clips, attach T-clips at the front of the new board, then fully tighten the previous set of T-clips. Add another deck board and repeat the process to the end of the deck.

4   Cover exposed deck board ends. Miter cut corners of the facing, and drill pilot holes ¾ the diameter of the screws. Attach with 3" galvanized deck screws.

1   Install the deck brackets along the top edge of each joist, alternating brackets from one side of the joist to the other in a continuous series. Secure the brackets with screws driven into the side of the joist.

2   Secure the deck boards by driving screws up through the bracket holes and into the joists. Depending on space constraints, these screws can be driven from above if necessary.

3   Continue installing all of the deck boards from below. When you reach the last board, you may need to install it from above for access reasons. Drive deck screws through the deck board and into the joists below. To maintain the hidden fastener appearance, counterbore the pilot holes for the screws and fill the counterbore with a plug cut from a piece of scrap decking.

1   Set a deck board into place on the joists, and slide a clip against it so the spacer tab touches the edge of the deck board. Drive a screw through the center hole of the clip and into the joist.

2   Drive a deck screw up through the plastic clip and into the deck board to secure it.

3   Position the next deck board against the clip's spacer tab, and drive a deck screw up through the clip to fasten it in place. One clip secures two deck boards at each joist location.

Stairs

HOW YOU BUILD STAIRS for your deck is perhaps the most tightly regulated portion of the building code related to decks. Whenever you are in doubt about measurements for deck stairs—or wondering if you even need to install stairs in the first place—consult the local building codes or local building inspector. Basically, designing deck stairs involves four calculations:

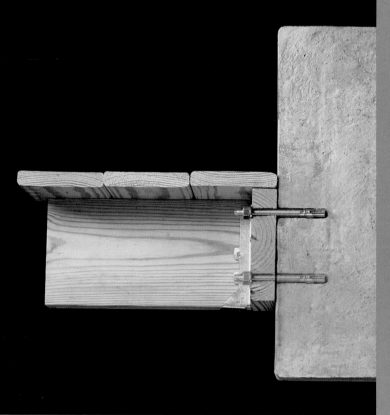

- **The number of stairs** depends on the vertical drop of the deck—the distance from the deck surface to the nearest ground level.

- **Rise** is the vertical space between treads. The proper rise prevents stumbling on the stairs. Most codes call for a maximum rise of 7¾ inches; a lower rise generally makes it easier to ascend or descend the stairs. The thickness of one tread is added to the space between steps to determine actual rise.

- **Run** is the depth of the treads, and is usually a minimum of 10 inches, although the deeper the tread, the more comfortable the stairs will be. Stair step thickness is also dictated by code and is usually a minimum of 1 inches, although most builders use 2× lumber for stair steps. A convenient way to build step treads is by using two 2 × 6s.

- **Span** is calculated by multiplying the run by the number of treads. The span helps you locate the end of the stairway so that you can properly position the posts.

Specifications for other elements such as the stringers and the method of attachment used to connect stairs to decking are also usually mandated in local codes. For instance, stringers normally have to be at least 1½ inches thick.

Although there are different ways to construct stairs, the same basic code requirements apply to any staircase used with a deck.

Tip: Materials for Deck Stairs

Most local building codes require that you use pressure-treated lumber for stairway posts and stringers. Install stair treads and risers cut from material that matches the surface decking. If possible, create treads that use the same board pattern as the decking. You may cover visible pressure-treated portions of the stairway with material matching the decking, too, or stain them to match the decking as closely as possible. Local codes may require handrails on stairways with three or more treads. Many codes also require a separate grippable handrail attached inside stair railings (on one side) in certain circumstances.

STAIRWAY STYLES

Open steps have metal cleats that hold the treads between the stringers. The treads on this stairway are built with 2 × 6s to match the surface decking.

Platform steps feature wide treads. Each step is built on a framework of posts and joists.

Boxed steps, built with notched stringers and solid risers, give a finished look to a deck stairway. Predrill the ends of treads to prevent splitting.

Long stairways sometimes require landings. A landing is a small platform to which both flights of stairs are attached.

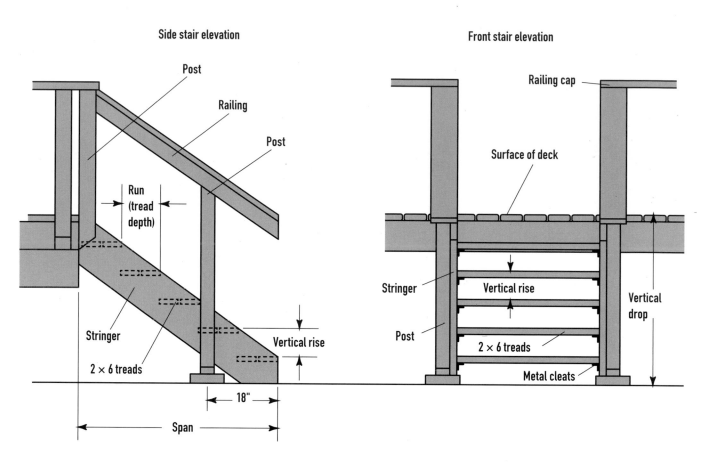

Side stair elevation

Front stair elevation

A common deck stairway is made from two 2 × 12 stringers and pairs of 2 × 6 treads attached with metal cleats. Posts set 18" back from the end of the stairway help to anchor the stringers and the railings. Calculations needed to build stairs include the number of steps, the rise of each step, the run of each step, and the stairway span.

FINDING MEASUREMENTS FOR STAIRWAY LAYOUT

			EXAMPLE (39" High Deck)
1. Find the number of steps: Measure vertical drop from deck surface to ground. Divide by 7. Round off to nearest whole number.	Vertical drop:		39"
	÷ 7 =		÷ 5.57"
	Number of steps: =		= 6
2. Find step rise: Divide the vertical drop by the number of steps.	Vertical drop: =		39"
	Number of steps: ÷		÷ 6
	Rise: =		= 6.5"
3. Find step run: Typical treads made from two 2 × 6s have a run of 11¼". If your design is different, find run by measuring depth of tread, including any space between boards.	Run:		11¼"
4. Find stairway span: Multiply the run by the number of treads. (Number of treads is always one less than number of steps.)	Run:		11¼"
	Number of treads:		× 5
	Span: =		= 56¼"

SIMPLE STAIRS: BUILDING A BOX-FRAME STEP

1 Construct a rectangular frame for the step using dimension lumber (2 × 6 lumber is standard). Join the pieces with deck screws. The step must be at least 36" wide and 10" deep. Cut cross blocks and install them inside the frame, spaced every 16".

2 Dig a flat-bottomed trench, about 4" deep, where the step will rest. Fill the trench with compactible gravel, and pack with a tamper. Set the step in position, then measure and attach deck boards to form the tread of the step.

1   Screw 2 × 4 furring strips against one side of the deck joists where the step joists will be installed. These strips provide an offset so the step joists will not conflict with the joist hangers attached to the beam. Use a reciprocating saw and chisel to make 1½"-wide notches in the rim joist adjacent to the furring strips. To maintain adequate structural strength, notches in the joists should be no more than 1½" deep.

2   Measure and cut step joists, allowing about 3 ft. of nailing surface inside the deck frame, and 10" or more of exposed tread. Make sure the step joists are level with one another, then attach them to the deck joists using deck screws. Cut and attach deck boards to the tread area of the step.

Tools & Materials

Tape measure
Circular saw
Screwgun
Hammer
Drill

⅛" twist bit
Pry bar
Chalk line
Jigsaw or handsaw
Decking boards

2½" corrosion-resistant
   deck screws
Galvanized common nails
   (8d, 10d)
Redwood or cedar facing boards

1   Use the stairway elevation drawings to find measurements for stair stringers and posts. Use a pencil and framing square to outline where stair stringers will be attached to the side of the deck.

2   Locate the post footings so they are 18" back from the end of the stairway span. Lay a straight 2 × 4 on the deck so that it is level and square to the side of the deck. Use a plumb bob or level to mark the ground at footing centerpoints.

3   Dig holes and pour the footings for posts. Attach metal post anchors to the footings and install the posts. Check with your building department to find out if 6 × 6 posts are now required.

continued

4   Lay out the stair stringers. Use tape to mark the rise measurement on one leg of a framing square, and the run measurement on the other leg. Beginning at one end of the stringer, position the square with tape marks flush to the edge of the board, and outline the rise and run for each step. Then draw in the tread outline against the bottom of each run line. Use a circular saw to trim the ends of the stringers as shown. (When cutting the stringers for stairs without metal cleats, just cut on the solid lines.)

5   Attach metal tread cleats flush with the bottom of each tread outline, using ¼" × 1¼" lag screws. Drill ⅛" pilot holes to prevent the screws from splitting the wood.

6   Attach angle brackets to the upper ends of the stringers using 10d joist hanger nails. Brackets should be flush with the cut ends of the stringers.

7   Position the stair stringers against the side of the deck, over the stringer outlines. Align the top point of the stringer flush with the surface of the deck. Attach the stringers by nailing the angle brackets to the deck with joist hanger nails.

8   Drill two ¼" pilot holes through each stringer and into each adjacent post. Counterbore each hole to a depth of ½", using a 1⅜" spade bit. Attach the stringers to the posts with ½ × 4" lag screws and washers, using a ratchet wrench or impact driver. Seal screw heads with silicone caulk.

9   Measure the width of the stair treads. Cut two 2 × 6s for each tread, using a circular saw.

10   For each step, position the front 2 × 6 on the tread cleat, so that the front edge is flush with the tread outline on the stringers.

continued

11   Drill ⅛" pilot holes, then attach the front 2 × 6 to the cleats with ¼ × 1¼" lag screws.

12   Position the rear 2 × 6 on the cleats, allowing a small space between boards. Use a 16d nail as a spacing guide. Drill ⅛" pilot holes, and attach the 2 × 6 to the cleats with ¼ × 1¼" lag screws. Repeat for the remaining steps.

STAIRBUILDING OPTION

Notched stringers precut from pressure-treated wood are available at building centers. Edges of cutout areas should be coated with sealer-preservative to prevent rot.

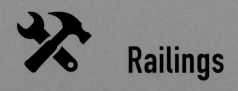

Railings

Tools & Materials

Tape measure
Pencil
Power miter saw
Drill
Twist bits (⅛", ⅜")
1⅜" spade bit
Combination square
Awl
Ratchet wrench
Caulk gun
Reciprocating saw
Circular saw
Jigsaw with wood-cutting blade
Miter saw
Level
Railing lumber (4 × 4s, 2 × 6s, 2 × 4s, 2 × 2s)
Clear sealer-preservative
½ × 4½" lag screws and 1⅜" washers
Silicone caulk
2½" corrosion-resistant deck screws
10d galvanized common nails

RAILINGS MUST BE STURDY and firmly attached to the framing members of the deck. Never attach railing posts to the surface decking. Check local building codes for guidelines regarding railing construction. Most codes require that railings be at least 36 inches above decking. Vertical balusters should be spaced no more than 4 inches apart. In some areas, a grippable handrail may be required for any stairway over four treads. Check with your local building inspector for the building codes in your area.

Railings are mandatory safety features for any deck that's more than 30" above grade. There are numerous code issues and stipulations that will dictate how you build your deck railings. Consult with your local building inspector for any code clarification you may need.

Refer to your deck design plan for spacing (A) and length of railing posts and balusters. Posts should be spaced no more than 6 ft. apart.

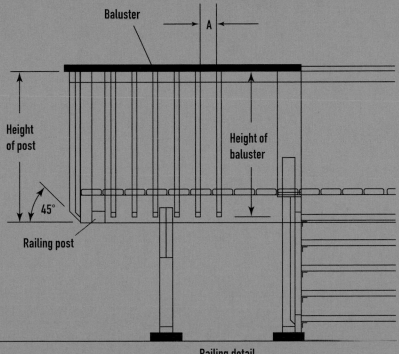

Baluster

A

Height of post

Height of baluster

45°

Railing post

Railing detail

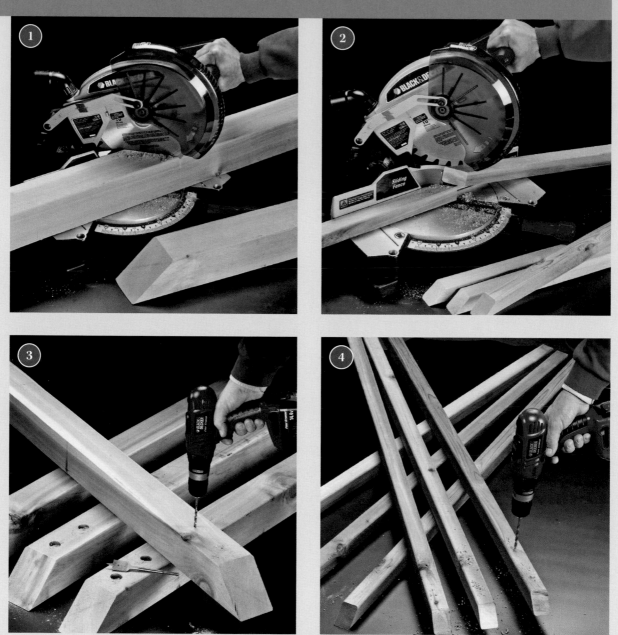

1   Measure and cut 4 × 4 posts using a power miter saw or circular saw. Cut the tops of the posts square, and cut the bottoms at a 45° angle. Seal cut ends of lumber with clear sealer-preservative.

2   Measure and cut the balusters for the main deck railing using a power miter saw or circular saw. Cut the tops of the balusters square, and cut the bottoms at a 45° angle. Seal cut ends of lumber with clear sealer-preservative.

3   Drill two ⅜" pilot holes spaced 2" apart through the bottom end of each post. Counterbore each pilot hole to ½" depth, using a 1⅜" spade bit.

4   Drill two ⅛" pilot holes spaced 4" apart near the bottom end of each baluster. Drill two ⅛" pilot holes at the top of each baluster, spaced 1½" apart.

5   Measure and mark the position of posts around the outside of the deck using a combination square as a guide. Plan to install a post on the outside edge of each stair stringer.

6   Position each post with the beveled end flush with the bottom of the deck. Plumb the post with a level. Insert a screwdriver or the ⅜" drill bit into the pilot holes and mark the side of the deck.

7   Remove the post and drill ⅜" holes into the side of the deck.

8   Attach railing posts to the side of the deck with ⅜ × 4½" lag screws and washers, using a ratchet wrench or impact driver. Seal the screw heads with silicone caulk.

continued

9   Measure and cut 2 × 4 side rails. Position the rails with their edges flush to the tops of posts, and attach to posts with 2½" corrosion-resistant deck screws.

10 Join 2 × 4s for long rails by cutting the ends at 45° angles. Drill ⅛" pilot holes to prevent nails from splitting the end grain, and attach the rails with 10d galvanized nails. (Screws may split mitered ends.)

11 Attach the ends of rails to the stairway posts, flush with the edges of the posts, as shown. Drill ⅛" pilot holes, and attach the rails with 2½" deck screws.

12 At a stairway, measure from the surface of the decking to the top of the upper stairway post (A).

13   Transfer measurement A to the lower stairway post, measuring from the edge of the stair stringer.

14   Position a 2 × 4 rail against the inside of the stairway posts. Align the rail with the top rear corner of the top post and with the pencil mark on the lower post. Have a helper attach the rail temporarily with 2½" deck screws.

15   Mark the outline of the post and the deck rail on the back side of the stairway rail.

16   Mark the outline of the stairway rail on the lower stairway post.

continued

17   Use a level to mark a plumb cutoff line at the bottom end of the stairway rail. Remove the rail.

18   Extend the pencil lines across both sides of the stairway post, using a combination square as a guide.

19   Cut off the lower stairway post along the diagonal cutoff line using a reciprocating saw or circular saw.

20   Use a jigsaw or miter saw to cut the stairway rail along the marked outlines.

21 Position the stairway rail flush against the top edge of the posts. Drill ⅛" pilot holes, then attach the rail to the posts with 2½" deck screws.

22 Use a spacer block to ensure equal spacing between balusters. Beginning next to a plumb railing post, position each baluster tight against the spacer block, with the top of the baluster flush to the top of the rail. Attach each baluster with 2½" deck screws.

23 For the stairway, position the baluster against the stringer and rail, and adjust for plumb. Draw a diagonal cutoff line on top of the baluster, using the top of the stair rail as a guide. Cut the baluster on the marked line, using a power miter saw. Seal the ends with clear sealer-preservative.

24 Beginning next to the upper stairway post, position each baluster tight against the spacer block, with the top flush to the top of the stair rail. Predrill and attach the baluster with 2½" deck screws.

continued

25 Position the 2 × 6 cap so that the edge is flush with the rail's inside edge. Drill ⅛" pilot holes and attach the cap to the rail with 2½" deck screws every 12". Drive screws into each post and into every third baluster. For long caps, bevel the ends at 45°. Drill ¹⁄₁₆" pilot holes and nail to the post with 10d nails.

26 At the corners, miter the ends of the railing cap at 45°. Drill ⅛" pilot holes, and attach the cap to the post with 2½" deck screws.

27 At the top of the stairs, cut the cap so that it is flush with the stairway rail. Drill ⅛" pilot holes and attach the cap with 2½" deck screws.

28   Measure and cut the cap for the stairway rail. Mark the outline of the post on the side of the cap, and bevel cut the ends of the cap. Position the cap over the stairway rail and balusters so that the edge of the cap is flush with the inside edge of the rail.

29   Drill ⅛" pilot holes and attach the cap to the rail with 2½" deck screws driven every 12". Also drive screws through the cap into the stair post and into every third baluster.

Curved Railings

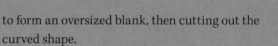

A curved cap rail is created from mitered segments of 2 × 12 lumber. After positioning the 2 × 12 segments end to end, the shape of the 6"-wide cap rail is outlined on the pieces. For a semicircle with a radius of up to 7 ft., four 2 × 12 segments will be needed, with ends mitered at 22½°. For a semicircle with a larger radius, you will need eight segments, with ends mitered at 11¼°.

Components of a curved railing include: vertical balusters attached to the curved rim joist, a top rail built from laminated layers of plywood, and a curved cap rail. The cap rail is constructed by laying out mitered sections of 2 × 12 lumber, marking a curved shape, and cutting it out with a jigsaw.

LAYING OUT AND CONSTRUCTING a curved railing requires a basic understanding of geometry and the ability to make detailed drawings using a compass, protractor, and a special measuring tool called a scale ruler. It is a fairly advanced technique, but the results are worth the effort. Making the top rail involves bending and gluing thinner strips of wood together around the deck's curved rim joist, which acts like a bending form. You'll need lots of medium-sized clamps on hand to hold the railing in the proper shape while it dries. The cap rail is formed by joining several mitered pieces of lumber together, end to end, to form an oversized blank, then cutting out the curved shape.

The method for constructing a curved cap rail shown on the following pages works only for symmetrical curves—quarter circles, half circles, or full circles. If your deck has irregular or elliptical curves, creating a cap rail is very difficult. For these curves, it is best to limit the railing design to include only balusters and a laminated top rail. Lastly, if this seems too complicated for your skills, you can opt for a composite curved railing, which can be made to order.

1   To create a curved top rail, use exterior glue to laminate four 1½"-wide strips of ⅜"-thick cedar plywood together, using the curved rim joist of the deck as a bending form. First, cover the rim joist with kraft paper for protection. Then, begin wrapping strips of plywood around the rim joist. Clamp each strip in position, starting at one end of the curve. The strips should differ in length to ensure that butt joints will be staggered from layer to layer.

2   Continue working your way around the rim joist, toward the other end. Make sure to apply clamps on both sides of the butt joints where plywood strips meet. Cut the last strips slightly long, then trim the laminated rail to the correct length after the glue has set. For extra strength, drive 1" deck screws through the rail at 12" intervals after all strips are glued together. Unclamp the rail, and sand the top and bottom edges smooth.

3   Install posts at the square corners of the deck. Then, cut 2 × 2 balusters to length, beveling the bottom ends at 45°. Attach the balusters to the rim joist with 2½" deck screws, using a spacer to maintain even intervals. Clamp the curved top rail to the tops of the balusters and posts, then attach it with deck screws.

4   After the top rail and balusters are in place, attach 2 × 2 top rails to the balusters in the straight sections of the deck. The ends of the straight top rails should be flush against the ends of the curved top rail. Now, measure the distance between the inside faces of the balusters at each end of the curve. Divide this distance in half to find the required radius for the curved cap rail.

continued

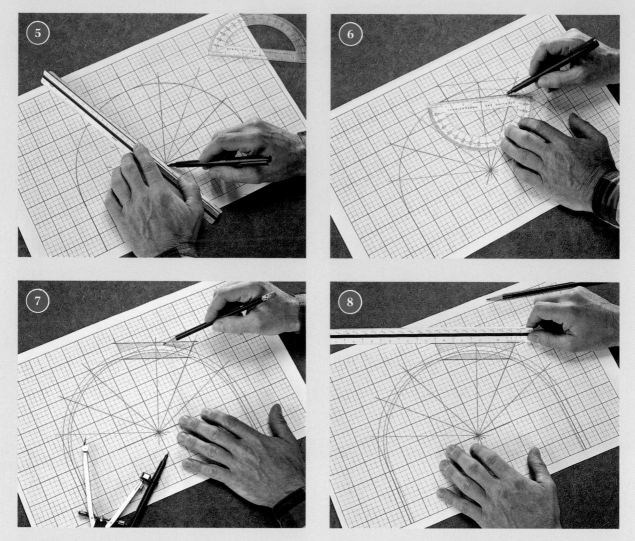

5   Using a scale of 1" to 1 ft., make a diagram of the deck. (A scale ruler makes this job easier.) First, draw the arc of the deck with a compass, using the radius measurement found in step 4. Divide the curved portion of the deck into an even number of equal sections by using a protractor to draw radius lines from the center of the curve. For a semicircular curve, it is usually sufficient to draw eight radius lines, angled at 22½° to one another. (For a deck with a radius of more than 7 ft., you may need to divide the semicircle into 16 portions, with radius lines angled at 11¼°.)

6   From the point where one of the radius lines intersects the curved outline of the deck, use the scale ruler to mark points 5½" above and 5½" below the intersection. From these points, use a protractor to draw perpendicular lines to the adjoining radius lines. The polygon outlined by the perpendicular lines and the adjoining radius lines represents the shape and size for all of the 2 × 12 segments that will be used to construct the cap rail.

7   Draw a pair of parallel arcs 5½" apart, representing the curved cap railing, inside the outline for the 2 × 12 segments. Shade the portion of the drawing that lies between the straight parallel lines and the two adjacent radius lines. This area represents the shape and size for each of the angled 2 × 12 segments. Measure the angle of the miter at the ends of the board; in this example, the segments are mitered at 22½°.

8   Measure the length of the long edge; this number is the overall length for each of the 2 × 12 segments you will be cutting. Using this highlighted area, determine how many segments you will need to complete the curve. For a semicircular curve with a radius of up to 7 ft., four segments are required, with ends mitered at 22½°. For curves with a larger radius, you need eight segments, with ends mitered at 11¼°.

9   Measure and mark 2 × 12 lumber for the cap rail segments, with ends angled inward at 22½° from perpendicular. Set the blade on your circular saw or tablesaw to a 15° bevel, then make compound miter cuts along the marked lines. When cut to compound miters, the segments will form overlapping scarf joints that are less likely to reveal gaps between the boards.

10   Arrange the cap rail segments over the curved deck railing, and adjust the pieces, if necessary, so they are centered over the top rail. When you are satisfied with the layout, temporarily attach the segments in place by driving 2" deck screws up through the curved top rail. Measure and install the 2 × 6 cap railing for the straight portion of the railing.

11   Temporarily nail or clamp a long sturdy board between the sides at the start of the curve. Build a long compass, called a trammel, by nailing one end of a long 1 × 2 to a 1 ft.-long piece of 1 × 4. Measure from the nail out along the arm of the trammel, and drill holes at the desired radius measurements; for our application, there will be two holes, 5½" apart, representing the width of the finished cap rail. Attach the 1 × 4 base of the trammel to the temporary board so the nail point is at the centerpoint of the deck rail curve, then insert a pencil through one of the holes in the trammel arm. Pivot the arm of the trammel around the cap rail, scribing a cutting line. Move the pencil to the other hole, and scribe a second line.

12   Remove the trammel, and unscrew the cap rail segments. Use a jigsaw to cut along the scribed lines, then reposition the curved cap rail pieces over the top rail. Secure the cap rail by applying exterior adhesive to the joints and driving 2½" deck screws up through the top rail. Use a belt sander to remove saw marks.

Deck Skirting

Tools & Materials

Measuring tape
Speed square
Circular saw
Miter saw
Power drill & bits
¾" exterior grade lattice panel
1 × 4 pressure treated lumber
2" galvanized finish nails
3" deck screws
Angle and T braces

Tip

You can even build in a storage space underneath the deck—a perfect location for lawnmowers, leaf blowers, and other yard equipment. Install a vinyl underdeck system to manage water run-off.

ELEVATED DECKS are often the best solution for a sloped yard or a multi-story house. A deck on high can also take advantage of spectacular views. But the aesthetic drawback to many elevated decks is the view from other parts of the yard. The supporting structure can seem naked and unattractive.

The solution is to install deck skirting. Skirting is essentially a framed screen attached to support posts. Skirting effectively creates a visual base on an elevated deck and adds a more finished look to the entire structure. It looks attractive on just about any deck.

There are many different types of skirting. The project here uses lattice skirting, perhaps the most common and easiest to install. But you can opt for solid walls of boards run vertically or horizontally, depending on the look you're after and how much time and money you're willing to spend. However, keep in mind that lattice allows for air circulation

underneath the deck. If you install solid skirting, you may need to add vents to prevent rot or other moisture related conditions under the deck. Codes also require that you allow access to egress windows, electrical panels, and other utilities under the deck, which may involve adding a gate or other structure to the skirting.

Regardless of the design, the basic idea behind building skirting is to create a supporting framework that runs between posts, with the skirting surface attached to the framework. Obviously, this provides the opportunity to add a lot of style to an elevated deck. The lattice skirting shown here is fairly easy on the eyes. If you choose to use boards instead, you can arrange them in intriguing patterns, just as you would design a showcase fence for your property. You can use wood skirting of the same species as the decking, or vary the material to create a more captivating look.

INSTALLING DECK SKIRTING

1   Determine the length of the skirting sections by measuring the space between posts. Measure on center and mark the posts. At corners, measure from the outer edge of the corner post to the center of the next post in line. Determine the height of the skirting by measuring from the top of a post to grade leaving at least 1" between the skirt bottom and ground.

2   Cut the top and side frame sections for the skirting from 1 × 4 pressure treated lumber. You can also use cedar or other rot- and insect-resistant material. Snap a chalk line 1" above the bottom of the post, and use a speed square to find the angle of the slope.

3   Cut the ends of the frame pieces to fit. Assemble the 1 × 4 frame using galvanized angle brackets.

4   Cut the ¾" lattice to dimensions of the frame, using a circular saw or jigsaw. Align the lattice on the back of the 1 × 4 frame, and screw the lattice to the frame about every 10".

5   Install each finished lattice skirting section as soon as it is assembled. Align the edges of the frame with the marks you've made on the posts and drill pilot holes through the front of the frame and lattice into the post. Screw the section to the post with 3" galvanized deck screws, using a screw at the top, bottom, and middle of the frame.

Deckbuilding Glossary

Baluster—a vertical railing member.

Batterboards—temporary stake structures used for positioning layout strings.

Beam—the main horizontal support for the deck, usually made from a pair of 2 × 8s or 2 × 10s attached to the deck posts.

Blocking—short pieces of lumber cut from joist material and fastened between joists for reinforcement.

Cap—the topmost horizontal railing member.

Cantilever—a common construction method (employed in some of the deck plans in this book) that involves extending the joists beyond the beam. The maximum overhang is specified in the Building Code.

Corner-post design—a construction method that incorporates posts at the outside edges of the deck, so the joists do not overhang the beam.

Decking—the floor boards of a deck (also known as deck boards).

End joists—the joists that are at each end of a series of parallel joists.

Face board—attractive wood, usually redwood or cedar, used to cover the rim joists and end joists.

Footing—a concrete pier that extends below the frost line and that bears the weight of the deck and any inset structures or furnishings.

Horizontal span—the horizontal distance a stairway covers.

Inset—an area of a deck that has been cut out to accommodate landscape features such as trees or to provide access to fixtures.

Joist—dimensional lumber, set on edge, that supports decking. Joists on attached decks hang between the ledger and rim joist.

Joist hanger—metal connecting pieces used to attach joists at right angles to ledger or header joists so that top edges are flush.

Ledger—a board, equal in size to the joists, that anchors the deck to the house and supports one end of the joists.

Open step—a step composed of treads mounted between stair stringers without any risers.

Post—a vertical member that supports a deck, stairway, or railing.

Post anchors—metal hardware for attaching deck posts to footings and raising the bottom of the post to keep it away from water. The end grain itself can be protected with sealer as added protection from rot.

Rim joist—a board fastened to the end of the joists, typically at the opposite end from the ledger. Rim joists attach to both ends of a free-standing deck.

Rise—the height of a step.

Riser—a board attached to the front of a step between treads.

Run—the depth of a step.

Span limit—the distance a board can safely cross between supports.

Stair cleat—supports for treads that are attached to stair stringers.

Stair stringer—an inclined member that supports a stairway's treads. A stair stringer may be solid, with treads attached to cleats mounted on the inside face, or cut out, with treads resting on top of the cutouts.

Tread—the horizontal face of each step in a stairway, often composed of two 2 × 6 boards.

Vertical drop—the vertical distance from the deck surface to the ground.

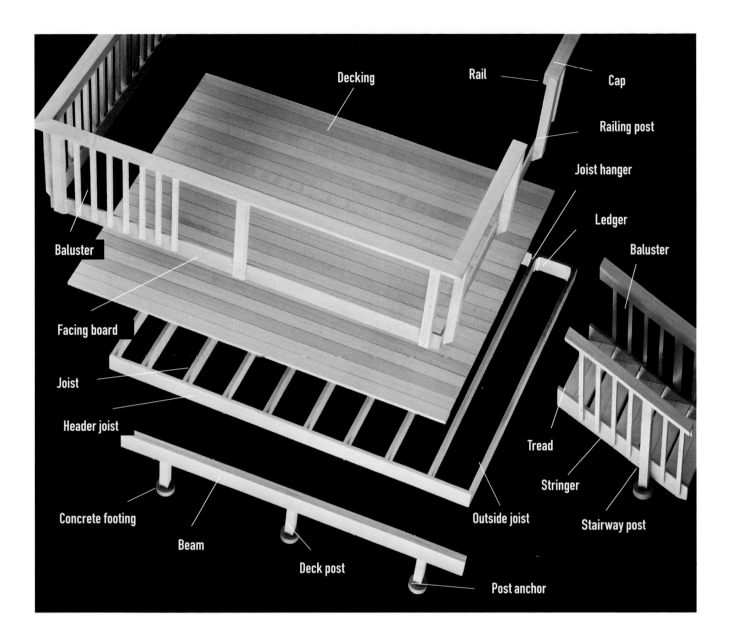

Decking

Rail

Cap

Railing post

Joist hanger

Ledger

Baluster

Baluster

Facing board

Joist

Header joist

Tread

Stringer

Concrete footing

Outside joist

Stairway post

Beam

Deck post

Post anchor

Metric Conversions

Metric Equivalent

Inches (in.)	1/64	1/32	1/25	1/16	1/8	1/4	3/8	2/5	1/2	5/8	3/4	7/8	1	2	3	4	5	6	7	8	9	10	11	12	36	39.4
Feet (ft.)																								1	3	3 1/12
Yards (yd.)																									1	1 1/12
Millimeters (mm)	0.40	0.79	1	1.59	3.18	6.35	9.53	10	12.7	15.9	19.1	22.2	25.4	50.8	76.2	101.6	127	152	178	203	229	254	279	305	914	1,000
Centimeters (cm)							0.95	1	1.27	1.59	1.91	2.22	2.54	5.08	7.62	10.16	12.7	15.2	17.8	20.3	22.9	25.4	27.9	30.5	91.4	100
Meters (m)																								.30	.91	1.00

Converting Measurements

To Convert:	To:	Multiply by:	To Convert:	To:	Multiply by:
Inches	Millimeters	25.4	Millimeters	Inches	0.039
Inches	Centimeters	2.54	Centimeters	Inches	0.394
Feet	Meters	0.305	Meters	Feet	3.28
Yards	Meters	0.914	Meters	Yards	1.09
Miles	Kilometers	1.609	Kilometers	Miles	0.621
Square inches	Square centimeters	6.45	Square centimeters	Square inches	0.155
Square feet	Square meters	0.093	Square meters	Square feet	10.8
Square yards	Square meters	0.836	Square meters	Square yards	1.2
Cubic inches	Cubic centimeters	16.4	Cubic centimeters	Cubic inches	0.061
Cubic feet	Cubic meters	0.0283	Cubic meters	Cubic feet	35.3
Cubic yards	Cubic meters	0.765	Cubic meters	Cubic yards	1.31
Pints (U.S.)	Liters	0.473 (Imp. 0.568)	Liters	Pints (U.S.)	2.114 (Imp. 1.76)
Quarts (U.S.)	Liters	0.946 (Imp. 1.136)	Liters	Quarts (U.S.)	1.057 (Imp. 0.88)
Gallons (U.S.)	Liters	3.785 (Imp. 4.546)	Liters	Gallons (U.S.)	0.264 (Imp. 0.22)
Ounces	Grams	28.4	Grams	Ounces	0.035
Pounds	Kilograms	0.454	Kilograms	Pounds	2.2
Tons	Metric tons	0.907	Metric tons	Tons	1.1

Converting Temperatures

Convert degrees Fahrenheit (F) to degrees Celsius (C) by following this simple formula: Subtract 32 from the Fahrenheit temperature reading. Then mulitply that number by 5/9. For example, 77°F - 32 = 45. 45 × 5/9 = 25°C.

To convert degrees Celsius to degrees Fahrenheit, multiply the Celsius temperature reading by 9/5, then add 32. For example, 25°C × 9/5 = 45. 45 + 32 = 77°F.

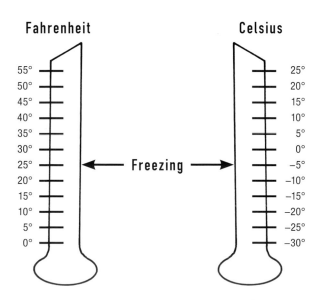

Index

First published in 2013 by Cool Springs Press, an imprint of the Quayside Publishing Group,
400 First Avenue North, Suite 400, Minneapolis, MN 55401

Cool Springs Press titles are also available at discounts in bulk quantity for industrial or sales-promotional use. For details write to Special Sales Manager at Cool Springs Press, 400 First Avenue North, Suite 400, Minneapolis, MN 55401 USA. To find out more about our books, visit us online at www.coolspringspress.com.

Library of Congress Cataloging-in-Publication Data

Homeskills. Building decks : all the information you need to design & build your own deck.
    pages cm
  ISBN 978-1-59186-581-0 (softcover)
  1. Decks (Architecture, Domestic)--Design and construction--Amateurs' manuals. I. Title: Home skills. Building decks. II. Title: Building decks.

  TH4970.H57 2013
  690'.184--dc23

            2013003984

Design Manager: Cindy Samargia Laun
Design and layout: John Sticha
Cover and series design: Carol Holtz

Printed in China
10 9 8 7 6 5 4 3 2 1

NOTICE TO READERS

For safety, use caution, care, and good judgment when following the procedures described in this book. The publisher cannot assume responsibility for any damage to property or injury to persons as a result of misuse of the information provided.

The techniques shown in this book are general techniques for various applications. In some instances, additional techniques not shown in this book may be required. Always follow manufacturers' instructions included with products, since deviating from the directions may void warranties. The projects in this book vary widely as to skill levels required: some may not be appropriate for all do-it-yourselfers, and some may require professional help.

Consult your local building department for information on building permits, codes, and other laws as they apply to your project.